Toxic Silence

D1526469

This book is part of the Peter Lang Humanities list.
Every volume is peer reviewed and meets
the highest quality standards for content and production.

PETER LANG
New York • Bern • Berlin
Brussels • Vienna • Oxford • Warsaw

William T. Hoston

Toxic Silence

Race, Black Gender Identity, and Addressing the Violence against Black Transgender Women in Houston

PETER LANG
New York • Bern • Berlin
Brussels • Vienna • Oxford • Warsaw

1-21-21
LB
#44.95

Library of Congress Cataloging-in-Publication Data

Names: Hoston, William T., author.
Title: Toxic Silence: Race, black gender identity, and addressing the violence against black transgender women in Houston / William T. Hoston.
Description: New York: Peter Lang, 2018.
Includes bibliographical references and index.
Identifiers: LCCN 2018006142 | ISBN 978-1-4331-5514-7 (paperback: alk. paper)
ISBN 978-1-4331-5599-4 (hardback: alk. paper)
ISBN 978-1-4331-5515-4 (ebook pdf) | ISBN 978-1-4331-5516-1 (epub)
ISBN 978-1-4331-5517-8 (mobi)
Subjects: LCSH: Transphobia—United States. | African American transgender people—Social conditions. | African American transgender people—Violence against—Texas—Houston. | African American transgender people—Texas—Houston—Social conditions.
Classification: LCC HQ77.965.U6 H67 2018 | DDC 306.76/8—dc23
LC record available at https://lccn.loc.gov/2018006142
DOI 10.3726/b13350

Bibliographic information published by **Die Deutsche Nationalbibliothek**.
Die Deutsche Nationalbibliothek lists this publication in the "Deutsche Nationalbibliografie"; detailed bibliographic data are available on the Internet at http://dnb.d-nb.de/.

The paper in this book meets the guidelines for permanence and durability of the Committee on Production Guidelines for Book Longevity of the Council of Library Resources.

© 2018 Peter Lang Publishing, Inc., New York
29 Broadway, 18th floor, New York, NY 10006
www.peterlang.com

Printed in Germany

To My Son
William Terrell Hoston Jr.
You were birthed to fulfill God's purpose for you
and take unconditional care of your mother.
You have the greatest mother in the world.
Daddy loves you.

You have given me a whole new appreciation for the color of life/ It was black, white, and red all over before you were born/ Watching you emerge from the womb/ Repainted my perspective/ From Parks to Lawrence to Barnes to Nelson/ You are a self-portrait of my own self/ A canvass of life/ Daddy's greatest masterpiece/ I love you/
~Ode to W.T.H. Jr.

I dedicate this book to the transgender community in the USA and globally. Please stop the transphobic discrimination, persecution, violence, and murders of transgender men and women.

A special dedication goes to Dr. Leon Pettiway who was well before his time in providing an academic voice to the black LGBTQIA community. More than twenty years ago, his books, *Honey, Honey, Miss Thang: Being Black, Gay, and on the Streets* (1996) and *Workin' It: Women Living Through Drugs and Crime* (1997), helped to revolutionize the intersection of the disciplines of black studies, sociology, criminology and criminal justice, political science, and gender and sexuality studies.

I think if trans folks don't stand up for themselves, nobody else is going to stand up for trans folks. If a trans person doesn't say I'm proud and I'm trans, then nobody is going to hop up there and say I'm proud and I'm trans for them.
~ Marsha P. Johnson, Transgender Activist

"Rest in Paradise" to the 49 LGBTQIA people who were senselessly murdered and 53 injured in the mass shooting at the Pulse nightclub in Orlando, Florida.
June 12, 2016

Stanley Almodovar III, 23
Amanda Alvear, 25
Oscar A Aracena-Montero, 26
Rodolfo Ayala-Ayala, 33
Antonio Davon Brown, 29
Darryl Roman Burt II, 29
Angel L. Candelario-Padro, 28
Juan Chevez-Martinez, 25
Luis Daniel Conde, 39
Cory James Connell, 21
Tevin Eugene Crosby, 25
Deonka Deidra Drayton, 32
Leroy Valentin Fernandez, 25
Simon Adrian Carrillo Fernandez, 31
Mercedez Marisol Flores, 26
Peter O. Gonzalez-Cruz, 22
Juan Ramon Guerroro, 22
Paul Terrell Henry, 41
Frank Hernandez, 27
Miguel Angel Honorato, 30
Javier Jorge-Reyes, 40
Jason Benjamin Josaphat, 19
Eddie Jamoldroy Justice, 30
Anthony Luis Laureano Disla, 25
Christopher Andrew Leinonen, 32

Alejandro Barrios Martinez, 21
Brenda Lee Marquez McCool, 49
Gilberto Ramon Silva Menendez, 25
Kimberly Morris, 37
Akyra Monet Murray, 18
Luis Omar Ocasio-Capo, 20
Geraldo A. Ortiz-Jimenez, 25
Eric Ivan Ortiz-Rivera, 36
Joel Rayon Paniagua, 32
Jean Carlos Mendez Perez, 35
Enrique L. Rios Jr., 25
Jean C. Nives Rodriguez, 27
Xavier Emmanuel Serrano Rosado, 35
Christopher Joseph Sanfeliz, 24
Edward Sotomayor Jr., 34
Yilmary Rodriguez Sulivan, 24
Shane Evan Tomlinson, 33
Martin Benitez Torres, 33
Jonathan Antonio Camuy Vega, 24
Juan P. Rivera Velazquez, 37
Franky Jimmy Dejesus Velazquez, 50
Luis S. Vielma, 22
Luis Daniel Wilson-Leon, 37
Jerald Arthur Wright, 31

CONTENTS

TABLES

ACKNOWLEDGMENTS

All praise to my Lord and savior, Jesus Christ. With Him, all things are possible. He has provided me with the four most influential women in my life, the late Mildred Hoston, the late Bertha-Mae Mitchell, Thelma C. Owens, and Janet Smith. I am a product of their hard work and sacrifice. In the words of Abraham Lincoln, "All that I am, or hope to be, I owe to my angel mother[s]."

I am indebted to the nine black transgender women who provided interviews to help make this book possible. Thank you. Thank you. Thank you. Thank you to Bobbie Golden, Arianna Gray, Venue Love, Naomi Mars, Jae Palmer, Sophie Rush, Mia Ryan, Jessica Sugar, and Alexandra Sweet. Two women, Sophie Rush and Mia Ryan, deserve special recognition for their input and suggestions from the beginning to the end of this book. I thank Mia Ryan very much for writing a foreword.

Thank you to Dr. Bakeyah S. Nelson who encouraged me to write this book. Thank you to the students, Randon R. Taylor, Anna A. Thomas, and Burgundy Anderson, who reviewed earlier drafts. I benefited from the many proofreading sessions and conversations. Many thanks go to Dr. Leon Pettiway for reading parts of the book in the beginning stages and offering sound advice. I am very thankful to the many anonymous reviewers and known reviewers who offered detailed and constructive criticisms and recommendations. Your recommendations helped this book to maintain intellectual integrity and spark constructive dialogue.

I would like to thank the former mayor of the city of Houston, Annise D. Parker, for her contribution to this project despite a busy schedule while exiting the mayoral seat. I know you will continue to be a strong LGBTQIA activist for many years to come.

To my beautiful and darling mother, Janet Smith, your examples of faith, courage, and sacrifice gave me much inspiration over the years to follow my dreams.

To my lovely wife, Cecilia Hoston, I love you. You have given my life such love, happiness, and joy. My wife and my son, William T. Hoston Jr., are my world. I want to thank both of them for giving my life more balance and purpose.

To my family and friends venturing to read this book who are devout Christians, see the world through a normative ideological lens, and will not agree with the words written on each page, please know that God directed me to write this book in the vein of black love. As the old folks say, "He put it on my heart" to write about the trials and tribulations of black transgender women because they are a part of the black community and must not be treated as outsiders.

Thank you to the transgender community for supporting me in the process of writing this book. I am a black cisgender man. Moreover, as a black cisgender man writing about the lived experiences of black transgender women, it was vital for me to be responsible for advocating, providing balance, and presenting principled criticisms in a manner most beneficial to the transgender community. To the best of my ability, I attempted to avoid cis-centric pitfalls. During the process of collecting information for this book, one black transgender woman who refused to participate said, "Thank you for asking, but I'm concerned about a book that examines black trans women's experiences being written for them by a black man instead of one of us." This sentiment reinforced the need for me to make sure that I put forth the effort to write a book that the black transgender community as a whole would be proud of when reading. Even after the completion of this book, I solicited the help of several of the black transgender women interviewed to read drafts of each chapter, provide constructive critique, and to make sure that this book has readability outside of academia. While this book may not encapsulate the spectrum of womanhood for all black transgender women, I hope that there is an appreciation for the effort.

I am grateful to Peter Lang Publishing for believing in this project. Thank you to Meagan K. Simpson, Michael Doub, and Jennifer Beszley for your editorial guidance and expertise.

To you whom I have not named, please know that even though you are not named in this book, I deeply appreciate what you have contributed to my life. Your contributions have helped this "Black boy fly."

FOREWORD

Words from Mia Ryan

William T. Hoston's book is one of the first of its kind to discuss the multiple intersections of the black trans experience. During a period in American history where trans people have had the most exposure, this book addresses the societal and cultural tug-of-war that continues to hinder the acceptance of black trans women. Most of all, it talks about the urgent need to safeguard black trans lives.

When I was born, I was medically assigned the sex of male. My parents gave me a name, Ryan Hogues. I was also required to assume a socially constructed racial and gender identity. Although I was born into this world assigned as both black and male, I understand that a fixed racial and gender identity does not indeed exist. Unfortunately, many people in our society do not see the world this way.

Growing up in Lamarque, Texas, a small town 50 miles south of Houston, I experienced constant bullying and teasing, which began during my elementary-school days. Even worse, I experienced abuse from my stepfather who believed he could beat the perceived "gay" out of me. The bullying and abuse continued into my teenage years. No one around me took the time to understand who I was as a person. Eventually, I left home at 13 years old in an attempt to escape the abuse.

When I left home, I sought refuge. I sought people who did not see race as real. I sought people who did not see gender as real. I wanted to immerse myself into a world where I could find out who I was. In the process of the coming out phase in my life, I wanted to be a part of a world that would accept me for whom I was becoming: A *black transgender woman*. I did not want to be a part of a world that still considered me a man because I have a penis. Those in this world use their fixation on genitalia as a weapon against my being and refuse to acknowledge my transition to becoming a woman.

The lived experiences of a trans person often depict how difficult and complicated it is to live in a society that believes our identities do not truly exist. For many trans people, our lives are no longer filled with family, friends, and loved ones. After the transition and lack of acceptance, many of us are forced to start over. Alone. For example, in my case, after I transitioned I lost connection with my family and friends. The greatest loss was that of my father and mother. Although these relationships are on the mend, the fabric of them is permanently torn. The two people who birthed me do not truly see me the way I desire for the world to see me.

Because so many people are attached to believing that biological sex is the same as gender, and also believe heterosexuality as the norm in our society, these views set the stage for non-acceptance, and we are often forced to survive by any means necessary. Consequently, many trans people, especially trans women, are placed in compromising circumstances that cost us our lives. I am optimistic that if those in mainstream society knew of the hardships and struggles that many trans people face, they would become allies and be more caring and compassionate.

It is my hope that this book will help to stop the transphobic violence perpetrated against black trans women. Therefore, I wish that members of society be less judgmental and more inclined to accept trans, gender non-conforming, and non-binary people so that senseless acts of violence, murders, and other forms of suffering cease. Our stories need to be told, not swept under the rug by politicians, law enforcement officials, or misrepresented in the media. This book is a step in the right direction, and I am happy that my truth will be told.

Mia Ryan
Author, Actress, Motivational Speaker, and Activist

· 1 ·

INTRODUCTION

Before I Was Trans, I Was Born Black

We're scared to death to be ourselves. We're human. We are a part of the so-called black community. I wish people would see us as that. We weren't confused black men who became black women. We were [black] women trapped in an unfamiliar body. That shouldn't make us a bull's eye.

—Venus Love

This book is primarily concerned with the toxic masculinity that threatens the humanity of black transgender women. The guiding framework centers on giving them a voice to address the increase of transphobic discrimination, violence, and murders. In that regard, the book focuses on three objectives: First, to better understand what it means to be a black transgender woman within the black community and in the larger American society. Second, to expand our knowledge and understanding of the societal and cultural impact of the black male-to-black female (MtF) transition on black masculinity and black femininity. Third and last, to address the deadly effects of toxic masculinity within the black community that leads to violence against black transgender women.

The above objectives are presented under the presumption that black LGBTQIA people and the lives they lead are a significant part of the black community and black American culture. As an extension of the Civil Rights

Movement and the fight for equal rights and protections, black people of all ages, creeds, color variations, sexes, national origins, religions, sexual orientations, gender identities, disabilities, marital statuses, and socioeconomic statuses are an interdependent group. The history of this group's identification with one another has relied on the generative power of black solidarity where individual blacks share a conscious fate with the larger black community. The United States of America's (USA) mistreatment of blacks throughout the centuries has been the impetus that has evoked intra-group ties to address discriminatory and racist practices. The main point is that, blacks would not have progressed to this point in history without acting as a collective group moving in a unified direction to achieve societal, cultural, and political liberation. Therefore, all black voices that resemble the diversity within the black community must be heard and their lives must matter if we are to achieve collective group actions that further the interests of blacks in American society.

The exploration of these objectives is timely and relevant for a number of reasons. First, the continued examination of black masculinity is needed to better understand the multi-dimensions of black male life. Following the election and presence of the first black president, Barack H. Obama, I, as well as many academics, found myself grappling with the following questions: *What does it mean to be a black male in the twenty-first century? Does Obama's presence have an impact on the black male identity?* Two of my previous books, *Black Masculinity in the Obama Era: Outliers of Society* (Hoston 2014) and *Race and the Black Male Subculture: The Lives of Toby Waller* (Hoston 2016), were written to get to the core of these questions.[1] Both of the books emphasize the importance of examining the social construction of black masculinity, the need to appreciate the diversity within the black male subculture[2], and the seriousness of protecting black human life in an American society that views black masculine bodies as social and political threats deserving of death.

As a backlash to the violence against black masculine bodies garnering national attention in recent years, the Black Lives Matter (BLM) movement was established to help socially, politically, and legally legitimize the value of black male lives. Black men in the USA are most violently under attack in two realms: white police-involved deaths and intra-racial violence. The deaths of unarmed black men by white law enforcement officers have been front and center in the black public consciousness. The names of Trayvon Martin, Michael Brown Jr., Jordan Davis, Eric Garner, Tamir Rice, Freddie Gray, Alton Sterling, Philando Castile, and a bevy of others shined a light on the rate of white police-involved deaths of unarmed black men. Take, for example, in

2015, black men made up roughly six and a half percent of the total USA population, yet an end of the year study by *The Guardian* revealed that they were nine times more likely than other Americans to be killed by police officers.[3]

In stark comparison, black men are killing each other at an alarming rate. Large proportions of intra-racial violence among black men occur every day in black communities. While such violence cultivated by age, gender, socio-economic status, and close geographical proximity is not a new phenomenon, the frequency in which it occurs identifies a disturbing trend within the black community. For example, Chicago, Illinois, or so inhumanely named in the twenty-first century, Chiraq, Killinois,[4] sees a disproportionate number of black men murdered due to gang-related violence over turf and drugs. At the end of 2016, the city of Chicago had seen a total of 762 murders[5] and more than 3,500 shooting incidents.[6] There was an average of two murders per day. When compared to 2015, which saw 468 murders, the city observed its largest murder increase in more than 60 years.

The fact is, not only are white law enforcement officers killing unarmed black men but black men are also killing other black men. One could possibly concede that the far greater problem is intra-racial violence among black men. However, the historical symbolism related to white police-involved deaths of unarmed black men stokes a fire in black Americans that reminds them of the gaudiness of a past history that dehumanized black masculine bodies. Despite this, both forms of violence against black men are equally important to combat in the mission to preserve black humanity.

The second reason of importance is that in the examination of the social construction of black masculinity, other groups such as black women and black lesbian, gay, bisexual, transgender, queer, intersex, and asexual (LGBTQIA) people who were carelessly excluded from the books mentioned above should have been included to provide a holistic viewpoint of black life.[7] Frameworks of inclusion for black women and black LGBTQIA people were needed to further our understanding of the multiple forms of oppression such as discrimination, racism, intra-racial connections and conflict, gender erasure, gender identity dismissal, and patriarchal violence that all reflect the totality of the black conscious struggle. To adopt black feminist scholar, bell hooks' (2004) term "imperialist white supremacist capitalist patriarchy," which explains the interlocking political systems of macro-level constructs, the struggle to end forms of oppression that affect black life is embedded in social structures of power. As a result, a worldview analysis is needed to better understand the multiple forms of oppression in all spheres of black life.[8]

In her book, *The Will to Change: Men, Masculinity, and Love*, hooks (2004) writes that the jargonistic term "imperialist white supremacist capitalist patri-archy," is used "to describe the interlocking political systems that are the foun-dation of our nation's politics. Of these systems the one that we all learn the most about growing up is the system of patriarchy" (pp. 17–18). The center of her argument is that each of these constructs is functioning simultaneously and acting as a web of oppression, however, patriarchy "insists that males are inherently [dominant]" and is the driving force of oppression "endowed with the right to dominate and rule over the weak and to maintain that domi-nance through various forms of psychological terrorism and violence" (p. 18). hooks contends that these macro-level constructs help to foster a system of patriarchy that first "demands of all males that they engage in acts of psychic self-mutilation" to "kill off the emotional parts of themselves," which helps to enable the exploitation and violence against black women (p. 66).

These macro-level constructs also incorporate micro-level constructs. At the micro-level, Kimberle Crenshaw (1989) in her groundbreaking analysis on "intersectionality" titled, *Demarginalizing the Intersection of Race and Sex*, argues that the intersecting social identities of race and gender, along with other forms of exclusion, leads to forms of discrimination and violence against black women. The foundation of her argument is that "boundaries of sex and race discrimination doctrine are defined respectively by white women's and black men's experiences" (p. 143). Crenshaw contends that it is imperative to apply an intersectional frame that examines the equation of these social iden-tities to best explain the dimensions of discrimination and violence against black women.[9] The line of demarcation that separates macro-level constructs and micro-level constructs has often coalesced. However, related to black women, adopting both macro-level constructs and micro-level constructs as a tool of explanation when appropriate, helps to explain the rate and various forms of discrimination and violence against these women.

One of the best-known national examples of the violence against black women during the BLM movement was the case of Sandra Bland. On July 13, 2015, her life was tragically altered after being stopped, abused, and arrested by a highway patrolman, Brian Encinia, for allegedly failing to use her turn signal. She committed suicide in her jail cell three days after being arrested. Bland's death brought more attention to state violence against black women, and the fact that she was one of five black women found dead in local police custody in July of 2015 alone.[10] The national outcry from Bland's death further challenged the need to obtain and secure social justice in the face of racialized state violence. During the same period, Daniel Holtzclaw, an ex-Oklahoma city law enforcement officer, targeted and sexually assaulted 13 black women from low-income neighborhoods while on duty in the community he patrolled. The defense attorney in the case attempted to label these black women as drug abusers and sex workers. Months later an all-white jury convicted Holtzclaw resulting in a 263-year prison sentence.[11]

Intimate partner violence (IPV) is another way in which black women experience victimization. IPV is defined as "physical violence, sexual violence, threats of physical or sexual violence, stalking and psychological aggression (including coercive tactics) by a current or former intimate partner" (Black et al. 2011, p. 37). According to a 2015 Violence Policy Center (VPC) report, 453 black women (28% of total women) were murdered in 2013.[12] Ninety-two percent of black women were victims of intra-racial murders committed by their spouse, an intimate partner, or a family member.[13] One heinous example is the 2016 death of 24-year-old, Joyce Quaweay, who was beaten to death by her 47-year-old boyfriend, Aaron Wright, along with his best friend, Marquis Robinson, who was a Temple University police officer. Wright beat Quaweay with his fists and a police baton while Robinson helped in restraining her because she refused to "submit to [Wright's] authority."[14] Police charged Wright with murder, aggravated assault, unlawful restraint, conspiracy to commit murder, and abuse of a corpse. Robinson was charged with conspiracy to commit murder, aggravated assault, and abuse of a corpse.[15] Sandra Bland's and Joyce Quaweay's cases are important examples of the dimensions of victimization that black women experience in American society and within the black community.

Third and finally, and the linchpin of this book, the objectives introduced are of great magnitude because black human beings who are members of both the black and LGBTQIA communities have become more at risk because of the systemic, institutional, and interpersonal underpinnings of racism, sexism, classism, homophobia, misogyny, and anti-trans attitudes and behaviors. The intersectionality of these constructs has amplified the level of discrimination and violence against this group. These constructs, when applied to black LGBTQIA people, are often driven by a practice of fostering a culture of secondary marginalization within the black community due to a lack of tolerance and acceptance (Cohen 1999) and the perpetual nature of anti-blackness from the mainstream LGBTQIA community.

In the realm of their everyday experiences, black LGBTQIA people are confronted with the pressure to adhere to societal, cultural, and gender norms

as heterosexual people. Such heteronormative thinking is tied to a rigid gender binary. According to Kitzinger (2005, p. 478), heteronormativity is viewed
as "the myriad ways in which heterosexuality is produced as a natural, unprob-
lematic, taken-for-granted phenomenon."[16] Such erroneous thinking assumes
that heterosexuality is the societal, cultural, and gender norm, whereas, those
who embody other sexualities and gender identities are aberrations within
American society.[17]

Richardson (2003, p. 64) in his description of the influence of compulsory heterosexuality on black Americans explains, "Any divergences from the
social norms of marriage, domesticity, and the nuclear family have brought
serious accusations of savagery, pathology, and deviance upon Black people."
Alternatively, Collins (2004), who in her work shows how whites have constructed black heterosexuality as pathological, did with the intent to control
sexual and gender images of blackness.

Under the LGBTQIA umbrella, the life experiences of each social group
have varied throughout history in their quest to achieve equal rights and protections. Despite LGBTQIA progress on the whole, according to national
reports and past literature, the acceptance and inclusion of transgender men
and women have lagged behind due to the social, cultural, and political sub-
jection of their gender identity. In the struggle for acceptance and inclusion,
transgender people who exhibit gender non-conforming identities and behaviors different from their birth identity, are labeled from conservative gender
ideologies as individuals who are participating in a destructive human act by
changing genders.

Transgender women (MtF), specifically, are stereotyped and observed by
the masses in American society as biologically born males who suffer from
gender dysphoria as a mental disorder. They are seen as males who dress in
women's clothing because they are either hypersexual monsters or want to
prey on women in public restrooms and locker rooms. These are all fictitious
claims that politicize the very nature of their being.

Many of these fictitious claims persist because transgender people are
systematically muted by a gendered American culture that views their transition as mentally and biologically abnormal. Claims like these are deemed
credible when political leaders like Republican Vice-President Mike Pence
endorses these ideas. He once advocated in 2000, while a member of the U.S.
Congress, to funnel money from HIV/AIDS research into LGBTQIA con-
version therapy.[18] Even more egregious, President Donald Trump is on record
in a 2017 *The New Yorker* article saying that Pence "wants to hang them all

[LGBTQIA people]."[19] Such ideologue in the political realm compromises the rights and protections of transgender people.

According to the 2011 National Transgender Discrimination Survey (NTDS) conducted by the National Center for Transgender Equality (NCTE) and the National LGBTQ Task Force, which was groundbreaking and the first survey of its kind, 63% of transgender people reported experiencing a serious act of discrimination.[20] The survey demonstrated that these acts of discrimination ranged from job loss due to bias, eviction due to bias, bullying, physical assault, sexual assault, homelessness, and incarceration due to gender identity. Forty-one percent of the respondents reported attempting suicide.[21] In December of 2016, the NCTE released the 2015 U.S. Transgender Survey (USTS), which is the largest and most comprehensive survey of transgender people to date.[22] This survey continued to show that transgender people face widespread discrimination.[23] Equally troubling is that the various forms of discrimination and violence continue to lead transgender people to attempt suicide. Forty percent of the respondents reported attempting suicide in their lifetime.[24]

These findings support, that in most cases, the life experiences of transgender people are fragmented in many ways. For instance, being unable to live comfortably in their transgender identity due to a lack of support from family and friends, harassment at school which can lead to dropout or poor performance, housing discrimination, denial of healthcare, the constant fear of losing employment, and even, being victimized by hate-based crimes at a disproportionate rate than nearly every other population in the USA. All of which, contributes to their heightened rate of suicide attempts.

The ability to secure justice for black transgender women who are systematically targeted has been difficult. These women represent an ostracized subgroup within both the black and the LGBTQIA communities. Generally speaking, within a black patriarchal community and culture, there is a rank and file approach of how societal and cultural issues and concerns are addressed by the community as a whole. Black elites are mainly responsible for determining which issues deserve the most attention. Thus, opposing the transphobic violence and murders of these women adds an ominous variable to this rank and file approach in determining whether it is "good, normal, and acceptable" for the community to help its "marginal group members" (Cohen 1999, p. 64). Consequently, this process inadvertently hurts, in general, the most vulnerable members of the community.

In the larger LGBTQIA community and culture, forms of anti-blackness plague black LGBTQIA people. The white LGBTQIA community may embrace racial and sexual stereotypes of racial and ethnic minority groups, which influences their perception of an individual's sexuality and gender identity (Barnard 2004). According to hooks in a one-on-one interview with *Trans-Scripts* when discussing anti-blackness in the context of black transgender people, she argues that "When most people think trans, they don't think black, they think white," which maintains such stereotypes.[25] Bey (2017), in his article that explores the concepts of black and trans, concurs with bell, however, adds that the integration of blackness within transness and vice-versa can lead to blackness-as-fugitivity, which harmfully places black human bodies in racial and gendered scripts.

Transgender scholar, Susan Stryker, who herself is transgender and has helped to revolutionize the field of transgender research, maintains that "Trans women of color get hit upside the head from a lot of different directions" when explaining their juxtaposition to white transgender women.[26] She describes, "First of all, there is misogyny. Then there's homophobia. And then you add the disparagement of black people on top of that, and that's a whole other level of disparagement and devaluation."[27] However, within the white community and given its culture, transgender women are somewhat more privileged because of the color of their skin and tend to be more isolated from many of the would-be forms of victimization. Moreover, there are more opportunities for employment outside of sex work, and more outward support from family and friends (Namaste 2000; Meyer 2008; Meyer 2010). In juxtaposing the lives of black transgender women and white transgender women, it is imperative not to belittle the negative circumstances that white transgender women do experience and assume that the benefit of privilege extends to the masses of these women. They are not shielded from mainstream normative ideas about sexuality, gender, and gender identity. However, it is an undeniable fact that black transgender women battle more forms of systemic, institutional, and interpersonal circumstances that make them societal and cultural outliers.

New black transgender voices have emerged to replace those of yesteryear who made significant strides to bridge the gap of gender identity understanding such as Miss Major Griffin-Gracy and Marsha P. Johnson who both participated in the 1969 Stonewall Riots in New York City, which served as the impetus for the formation of the modern LGBTQIA movement.[28] Black transgender activists like Andrea Jenkins,[29] Janet Mock, Laverne Cox, Tracey Norman, Monica Roberts, Fran Watson, Dee Dee Watters, Mia Ryan, Elle Hearns, Cherno Biko, and Raquel Willis have emerged to fight on behalf of black transgender women in the USA.

In a 2016 HBO documentary, *The Trans List*, Griffin-Gracy makes the case that despite progress for the LGBTQIA community as a whole, more change is needed to advance the specific agenda of the transgender community. Using the Stonewall Riots as an example, she stated, "To me, T [within the LGBTQIA acronyms] should have been first. We were there doing most of the fighting. So let's start there and then let's get the gay and lesbian and bi [equal rights and protections addressed]."[30] She also expressed that past meaningful efforts were diminished due to the larger patriarchal and heteronormative frames that preserve the remembrance of white transgender archives. Ware (2017), in his article that examines the erasure of racialized and indigenous histories from white trans archives, argues that we must begin with black trans and queer history to best weigh the influence and significance of black LGBTTI2QQ people.[31] The power and privilege of selective remembrance that Ware describes in the article is the impetus for the marginalization that maintains a divide for the lack of black transgender acknowledgement in the larger LGBTQIA community.

A New Communal Epidemic: Black Transphobic Violence and Murders

In recent years, more cases of transphobic violence and murders against transgender women, specifically black transgender women, have gained national attention (see Table 1.1). For example, in 2015, the number of murders recorded hit a historic high. The National Coalition of Anti-Violence Programs (NCAVP) reported that there were a record total of 22 transgender women murdered.[32] Black transgender women accounted for 17 of the 22 deaths (77%) in the USA (see Table 1.2).[33] This marked the most black transgender women murdered within a single year on record to date.[34]

An awful example of the transphobic violence and murders of black transgender women occurred in Detroit, Michigan. Between 2011 and early 2016, seven transgender women and/or gender non-conforming individuals were murdered in the city.[35] In 2015, two black transgender women, Ashton O'Hara and Amber Monroe, and one gender non-conforming individual were murdered near Palmer Park, an area known as a black LGBTQIA hangout spot and for transgender sex work.[36] In the summer of 2014, three black transgender women were shot near the park, with one being fatally shot.[37] Because of these acts of violence, black transgender women near Palmer Park feared that random

Table 1.1. The Deaths of Transgender Women, 2012–15.

2012	2013	2014	2015
1. Crain Cornaway	1. Evon Young	1. Yaz'min Shancez	1. Papi Edwards
2. Deoni Jones	2. Cernia Dove	2. Kandy Hall	2. Lamia Beard
3. Agnes Hernandez	3. Kelly Young	3. Zoraida Reyes	3. Tyra Underwood
4. Coko Williams	4. Ashley Sinclair	4. Tiffany Edwards	4. Yazmin Vash Payne
5. Tyrell Jackson	5. Islan Nettles	5. Mia Henderson	5. Taja Gabrielle DeJesus
6. Paige Clay	6. Dominique Newburn	6. Alejandra Leos	6. Penny Proud
7. Brandy Martell	7. Eyricka Morgan	7. Aniya Parker	7. Kristina Gomez Reinwald
8. Lorena Xtravaganza	8. Jessica Bringas	8. Shelly Hiliard	8. Keyshia Blige
9. Tracey Johnson	9. Melony Smith	9. Ashley Sherman	9. London Kiki Chanel
10. Tiffany Gooden	10. Betty Skinner	10. Breana Fowler	10. Mercedes Williamson
11. Deja Johnson	11. Brittany Stergis	11. Deshawnda Sanchez	11. Jasmine Collins
12. Kendall Hampton			12. Ashton O'Hara
13. Kyra Cordova			13. India Clarke
14. January Lapuz			14. K.C. Haggard
15. Rene Hidalgo Hernandez			15. Shade Schuler
			16. Amber Monroe
			17. Kandis Capri
			18. Elisha Walker
			19. Tamara Dominguez
			20. Keisha Jenkins
			21. Zella Ziona
			22. Mya Hall
N=15	N=11	N=11	N=22

Source: The National Coalition of Anti-Violence Programs (NCAVP)

Table 1.2. The Deaths of Transgender Women, 2015.

1. Papi Edwards, 20, Black, Louisville, Kentucky
2. Lamia Beard, 30, Black, Norfolk, Virginia
3. Tyra Underwood, 24, Black, Tyler, Texas
4. Yazmin Vash Payne, 33, Black, Van Nuys, California
5. Taja Gabrielle DeJesus, 33, Hispanic, San Francisco, California
6. Penny Proud, 21, Black, New Orleans, Louisiana
7. Kristina Gomez Reinwald, 46, Hispanic, Miami, Florida
8. Keyshia Blige, 33, Black, Aurora, Illinois
9. London Kiki Chanel, 21, Black, Philadelphia, Pennsylvania
10. Mercedes Williamson, 17, Hispanic, George County, Mississippi
11. Jasmine Collins, 32, Black, Kansas City, Missouri
12. Ashton O'Hara, 25, Black, Detroit, Michigan
13. India Clarke, 25, Black, Tampa, Florida
14. K. C. Haggard, 66, White, Fresno, California
15. Shade Schuler, 22, Black, Dallas, Texas
16. Amber Monroe, 20, Black, Detroit, Michigan
17. Kandis Capri, 35, Black, Phoenix, Arizona
18. Elisha Walker, 20, Black, Smithfield, North Carolina
19. Tamara Dominguez, 36, Hispanic, Kansas City, Missouri
20. Keisha Jenkins, 22, Black, Philadelphia, Pennsylvania
21. Zella Ziona, 21, Black, Gaithersburg, Maryland
22. Mya Hall, 27, Black, Baltimore, Maryland

acts of hate-based violence such as "robberies, knifings, sucker-punchings, more homicides, dismemberment, charred bodies, trans women being shoved out of moving cars, and other acts of violence" would affect them as well.[38]

Many of the black transgender women in Detroit and within the USA who were murdered in 2015 worked in the sex trade profession. According to a 2015 joint report on transgender experiences in the sex trade profession led by the NCTE, 44% of black transgender women and 33% of Latina transgender women were more likely to engage in sex work than their white counterparts.[39] As laborers in this profession, the majority of these women are reluctant to report incidents of abuse, harassment, and violence to law enforcement officers for two major reasons: First, black transgender women fear being criminalized for sex work. Second, according to the 2011 NTDS, 38% of black transgender people reported being harassed by law enforcement officers and 51% felt discomfort with seeking their assistance.[40]

The mounting national violence and murders against the transgender community prompted U.S. Representative Mike Honda of California (D-17), whose granddaughter is transgender, to call a congressional forum on November 17, 2015, and launch the Transgender Equality Task Force (TETF) to address this growing epidemic.[41] During this forum, Harper Jean Tobin, the Director of Policy for the NCTE, who is transgender, said in her presentation to congressional members that, "We know the numbers [of violence and murders] are far higher than that [reported]. Even the FBI will admit the data are collected and reported so inconsistently as to render them almost meaningless."[42]

The black transgender women interviewed for this book claim that black cisgender men commit the vast majority of transphobic violence and murders against them. Cisgender, the opposite of transgender, is a term used to describe individuals whose medically birth-assigned sex matches their gender identity.[43] The women interviewed believe that a traditional gender norm gives rise to a toxic masculine makeup, which is bred in a patriarchal system of male domination influenced by the authoritative nature and structure of white supremacy. As an offspring of hegemonic masculinity (i.e., dominant masculinity) that is connected to heteropatriarchy, where men adhere to a cultural script of primacy over women, toxic masculinity is a rebellious form of manhood practiced mostly by black men in low socioeconomic environments and utilizes violence to legitimize masculinity (see Harris 2000, 2011).[44]

According to (Kupers 2005, p. 714), toxic masculinity is "the constellation of socially regressive male traits that serve to foster domination, the devaluation of women, homophobia, and wanton violence." Moreover, feminist activist, Bailey Poland, defined toxic masculinity as:

> The version of masculinity that values physical strength and aggression, downplays overall emotional well-being and expression, connects men's value to domination by force and sexual prowess and often finds its voice in misogyny, homophobia, and transphobia.[45]

When applied to black transgender women, toxic masculinity is most put on display when black cisgender men are motivated by hate, engage in intimate personal relationships with these women, or solicit their services as transgender sex workers. Afterwards, they rationalize their decision and their sexual involvements with these women, which often leads them to question their masculinity, and as a response, use violence as a defense mechanism to regain dominance, control, and gain a psychological sense of wholeness. This allows them to subdue their attraction for these women and return to a very strict idea of gender norms. Toxic masculinity, in this manner, is harmful to the humanity of black transgender women.[46]

The black transgender women interviewed unanimously agreed that black cisgender men through hate-based violence, intimate partner violence, and violence against transgender sex workers, murder a disproportionate number of black transgender women. For instance, Jessica Sugar, a 31-year-old participant, who works in the sex trade profession, described:

> Excuse my language, but some of these black cis men will fuck you, kill you, and leave you to die. I do not accept inquires from black cis men. I state that on my [Backpage. com] profile. We are a novelty to them. Once it wears off, their masculinity kicks in and we become the scum of the earth. If we date them, there is a chance we will die. If we service them, there is a chance [we will die]. We can't live safe.

Shugrue dos Santos (2012) supports her statement. Her research on intimate partner violence within the lesbian, gay, bisexual, transgender, queer, and HIV-affected (LGBTQH) communities, found that transgender people are at a much higher risk for intimate partner violence and sexual violence (SV) than non-transgender people in given situational and cultural contexts.

A different form of victimization against black transgender women comes from law enforcement officials who "misgender" these women after their deaths. While statistics related to the harassment, assault, and criminalization of these women have been recorded somewhat, gender misidentification is a serious concern in the transgender community because it contributes to the difficulty in quantifying the total number of transgender deaths each year. In the deaths of Keyshia Blige, Shade Schuler, Mya Hall, and others during 2015, the failure of law enforcement officials to either investigate, accurately report their gender identity, or mere refusal of these officials to acknowledge the victim's gender identity based on the patriarchal way in which they perform their jobs often delayed or negated proper identification of these women when struggling to secure justice.

In July of 2015, Shade "Ms. Shade" Schuler, a black transgender woman from Dallas, Texas, was the 13th transgender woman to be reported murdered for the year. She was shot and abandoned in a vacant field. Her badly decomposed body partly prolonged the proper identification of her body for nearly two weeks after she was found.[47] In the aftermath of her death, the Dallas police department and news outlets misidentified Schuler as a male when referring to her death to the public.

The death of Shade Schuler prompted black transgender activists Monica Roberts, who herself is a black transgender woman, and Fran Watson, both from Houston, Texas, to set up a petition on the White House website

to encourage former President Barack H. Obama to launch a formal investigation into the issues associated with transgender violence and murders.[48]
Unfortunately, their petition failed to garner a sufficient amount of signatures.

The Black Lives Matter (BLM) Response

Three black women, Alicia Garza, Patrisse Cullors and Opal Tometi, helped
to pioneer the BLM movement. This proactive, decentralized movement has
become an influential voice for the black community.[49] However, the movement, while now serving as one of the most socially and culturally significant
since the Civil Rights era, only contains a small fraction of black people from
within the community working together to secure justice for the community
as a whole.

Black participation in the BLM movement as a whole has been stagnant
for a number of reasons. There are unfounded claims that certain factions of
the black community are reluctant to fully support the BLM movement due
to: (1) the movement being started by three black feminists, (2) two of its
founders, Alicia Garza and Patrisse Cullors, identify as queer, (3) the movement rejects the hierarchical style of patriarchal leadership, and (4) the social
institution of the black church is not the anchor in catapulting their message.
In stark contrast, their leadership is deemed refreshing to some due to the sexism within the Civil Rights era that often silenced the voices of great women
activists such as Fannie Lou Hamer and Ella Baker.

Former columnist Barbara Reynolds, and a member of the 1960s Civil
Rights Movement, wrote her dissent to the BLM movement in a *Washington
Post* article:

> Many in my crowd admire the cause and courage of these young activists but fun-
> damentally disagree with their approach. Trained in the tradition of Martin Luther
> King Jr., we were nonviolent activists who won hearts by conveying respectability and
> changed laws by delivering a message of love and unity. BLM seems intent on reject-
> ing our proven methods. This movement is ignoring what our history has taught.[50]

Moreover, while it is consciously assumed that there should be solidarity from
non-BLM members that would extend activism throughout the black community as a cultural norm, such communal solidarity is needed to further overall
progress. Ultimately, a greater majority of the people within the black community must want to work as agents of social change to make the community a
safer cultural haven for all black lives, which includes black transgender people.

One of the central arguments presented in this book is that the black community and the BLM movement must not solely be responsive to the torrent relationship between white law enforcement officers and unarmed black men; but also, be responsive to the victimization of black women, black LGBTQIA people, and all forms of internal community violence that ravages the black community. Are the black men senselessly murdered from intra-racial violence devalued in the BLM movement? Are black women devalued in the BLM movement? Are black LGBTQIA people and their lives devalued in the BLM movement? All of these questions carry significant weight since the black community has inoculated, to a large degree, the BLM movement as a de facto homogenized face and voice of black solidarity for a community whose historical mission has always been to combat structural and cultural inequality while attaining equal rights and protections for all of its members.

Lost in the early origins of the BLM movement were any substantive dis-cussions about black women and their rights and protections. Even though three black women founded the movement, the desire to urgently address the victimization of black men was prioritized over the needs of black women. hooks, in the interview with *Trans-Scripts*, maintained that:

> I find a lot of feminists/women saying "yeah, but the subtext is really black male lives matter"—that the killing of black women never seems to be relegated to that equal place of the killing of black men and the fact is black women are being killed everyday in all kinds of ways ... Any black man's life has so much more value than a black female life.[51]

Other black feminists also shared hook's position. After the jail suicide of Sandra Bland, the BLM movement, who had already adopted a universal hash tag "#BlackLivesMatter," eventually pushed for another hash tag "#Say-HerName" to make the movement more gender-inclusive and to bring more awareness to black female victims.[52] As the deaths of black transgender women gained national spotlight, another universal hash tag "#BlackTransLivesMat-ter," was also embraced to address this epidemic, which called for more trans-gender advocacy through political, legislative, and communal channels.

In response to the murders of black transgender women, one of the found-ing members of the BLM movement, Alicia Garza, who is queer and dates a transgender man, not only advocated for more space in the movement for all black people, including black transgender people, but also made the point that, "[Black Trans Lives Matter] speaks most directly to the marginaliza-tion and disenfranchisement of trans people within the black community."[53] During the height of these black transgender murders in mid-2015, she wrote on her Facebook page, "Each one of these women should still be alive—but they are not because the lives of trans women are seen as disposable."[54] Garza went on to add, "The murders of trans women alongside the multiple other forms of violence that trans women experience must be elevated to the level of conversation that the murders of cis Black men now occupy."[55] Garza closed her post by stating, "It cannot constantly be the job of trans women to constantly remind us that their lives matter too. The liberation of Black people as a whole depends on the liberation of Black trans folks. None of us are free until all of us are free."[56]

In 2016, amidst the backlash from the black transgender community, the BLM movement introduced an LGBTQIA agenda:

> We are committed to embracing and making space for trans brothers and sisters to participate and lead. We are committed to being self-reflexive and doing the work required to dismantle cis-gender privilege and uplift Black trans folk, especially Black trans women who continue to be disproportionately impacted by trans-antagonistic violence.[57]

Despite pledging to be transformative and working to address the "trans-antagonistic violence," some of the black transgender women interviewed believe the action of the BLM movement fails to address one of the more critical mitigating factors of this epidemic: black cisgender men who murder black transgender women.

Black transgender women's inclusion into the societal and cultural responsiveness of the black community and the BLM movement revolves around the need for equal rights and protections, which must be given for their human survival and well-being. It can be argued that black transgender women are first human beings, who represent every possible human, physical form (i.e., from being medically assigned the sex of male at birth, from being identified as a black gay man, from transitioning to a black transgender woman, and from being perceived as a black cisgender woman). Thus, there is a fluid and complex viability to their humanity.

Why the Time Is Now?

Black people of varying gender identities and sexual orientations compromise the black community. In that regard and according to, this textured analysis argues that the humanity of Michael Brown Jr., Sandra Bland, and Shade "Ms. Shade" Schuler are all intertwined. The truth is that, whether you are

Michael Brown Jr., Sandra Bland, or a black transgender woman self-identified as Ms. Shade, you can be gunned down in the middle of the street by a white police officer, found dead in a jail cell after failing to use your turn signal, or shot and abandoned in a vacant field for nearly two weeks.

The deaths of Michael Brown Jr. and Sandra Bland were catapulted into the national spotlight and garnered enormous support from the black community and the BLM movement. In stark contrast, the death of Ms. Shade who was the 13th transgender woman murdered in 2015 should have garnered equal attention. However, it did not. Violence and murders against these women were largely ignored, especially within the black community. Much of the disregard for the humanity of black transgender woman centers on the patriarchal and heteronormative frames within the black community and in the larger American society that dehumanizes their existence.

The quest to address the aforementioned objectives introduces the following questions to guide this book: *What are the implications for black transgender women medically assigned the sex of male at birth but have chosen to exercise their right to identify as a transgender and/or gender non-conforming person within the black community, which has historically shown a propensity to promote a toxic masculinity within the context of a black patriarchal culture and suppress any form of femininity in black men? How, then, do black transgender women live as black women within a black patriarchal culture that facilitates toxic masculinity? Can the black community and Black Lives Matter movement progress in a unified direction to protect the humanity of black transgender women?*

The goal of this book is to widen the discussion on black transgender women, and by extension, to expand our understanding of black masculinity and black femininity. Some within the black community and in the larger American society view these women as the more ill-fitting pieces of our gendered American culture. The concern for their human survival and well-being is the charge and significance for writing this book. The aspiration is to preserve the dignity of their humanity by analyzing their lived experiences in a gendered American culture that works at every turn to marginalize their human existence.

Overview of the Book

Toxic Silence contributes to a growing body of transgender scholarship. This book examines the patriarchal and heteronormative frames within the black community and in the larger American society, which propels the toxic masculinity that violently castigates and threatens the collective embodiment of black transgender women in the USA. Such scholarship is needed to shed more light on the transphobic violence and murders against this understudied group. Little is known about the societal and cultural issues and concerns affecting black transgender women and how their gender identity is met with systemic, institutional, and interpersonal roadblocks. During a time period in American history defined by *Time Magazine* as, "The Transgender Tipping Point,"[58] black transgender women have emerged as social, cultural, and political subjects to advance our understanding of the lives of people who identify as a part of both the black and LGBTQIA communities.

Chapter 2, "The Black Trans Identity," attempts to offer an expanded cultural perspective of the lived experiences of black transgender women, and explores both their gender identity and their ability and willingness to fit, or not fit, into mainstream black communal life. Their sense of identity within the black community stands as the assemblage of the social constructions of race and gender identity, socioeconomic status, and a biased communal perception influenced by the ideological indicators of religion, morality, and ethics. Drawing on survey data and in-depth interviews, this chapter provides an empirical analysis of black cisgender attitudes towards black transgender women.

Chapter 3, "Black Transphobic Violence and Murders," focuses on the transphobic violence and murders of black transgender women. Even with the total number of murders in recent years, little is known about the circumstances surrounding the deaths of these women. This chapter applies an intersectional approach to explore the situational and cultural contexts that lead to the transphobic violence and murders of these women.

Chapter 4, "Black Trans Voices," presents a case study of the life histories of three black transgender women from Houston, Texas. Drawing on participant observations and in-depth interviews, this chapter provides a rich and engaging description about the lived experiences of these women. It seeks to give a more complete picture of the MtF transition of black transgender women as it examines the extensive systemic, institutional, and interpersonal circumstances that affect these women. The objective is to discover whether the oppressive constructs of race, sexuality, and gender identity, and the socioeconomic status said to exist in the dominant norms of heterosexuality lead the majority of transgender women to live on the margins of society.

Finally, Chapter 5, "Black Trans Liberation," offers a summary of the overall findings and argues that it is critical to create more societal and cultural spaces for black transgender women to foster acceptance and inclusion. To end the book, provided are solution-based recommendations to propel equal rights and protections for black transgender women and to improve the generative power of black solidarity within the black community and culture.

Research Design and Data

The setting for examining the toxic masculinity that threatens the humanity of black transgender women is the city of Houston, Texas. With a population of over two million people, this liberal-leaning city within a conservative state is the fourth most populous in the USA. Houston contains a very diverse population. According to the 2010 U.S. Census Bureau, whites accounted for 50.5% of the population, with non-Hispanic whites making up 25.6% of the total population. In terms of the city's racial and ethnic population, 43.8% are Hispanic, 23.7% are black, and 6% are Asian.

The city of Houston is a suitable contextual laboratory to study the lives of black transgender women for the following reasons: First, from 2010 to 2016, the city was led by a Democratic mayor, Annise D. Parker, who was openly lesbian in office, and who aggressively pushed for measures such as the Houston Equal Rights Ordinance (Ord. No. 2014–530), commonly known as HERO, which, among other things, would have provided transgender protections in public accommodations such as entering gender-preferred bathrooms.[59] Before and during her time in the mayoral seat, Parker was a staunch LGBTQIA activist, which helped to create a more LGBTQIA-friendly atmosphere of acceptance and inclusion in the city. Second, Houston ranks among the top metropolitan cities with a large LGBTQIA population.[60]

In an interview with the former mayor, during the beginning stages of writing this book, Parker explained why there were increasing numbers of black transgender women being murdered in American society. She stated that:

> Society is still largely ignorant of what it means to be transgender. The economic and social impact of transitioning can be financially and psychologically devastating. Transgender women are often dehumanized and the lack of knowledge means that societal taboos against harassing the minority are ignored. Too many transgender women are forced into the sex trade [profession], where they become particularly vulnerable targets.[61]

This study of the transphobic violence and murders affecting black transgender women employs a multi-method approach that includes both qualitative and quantitative methods. The qualitative analysis involves the use of in-depth interviews and participant observations. Due to the scarcity of research on black transgender women and limited access to willing participants in such studies, using a qualitative methodological approach was most appropriate. A purposeful sample of nine black transgender women from the city of Houston, Texas—Bobbie Golden, Arianna Gray, Venue Love, Naomi Mars, Jae Palmer, Sophie Rush, Mia Ryan, Jessica Sugar, and Alexandra Sweet—is the primary method of data collection (Patton 2002; See Appendix A.1 for a full description). Six of the nine black transgender women interviewed work in the sex trade profession. The selection of these women was based on willing participation and availability, and not to further stigmatize transgender women as a whole as mere sex workers. Due to the sensitivity of the subject matter, the research assured participants' anonymity to the women. The use of a purposeful sample allowed for a closer look at these black transgender women and their lived experiences.

This qualitative approach is combined with survey data from black cisgender people in the greater Houston metropolitan area. Such data is collected to gauge their attitudes toward black transgender women. These different approaches allow the triangulation of data to give more insight and credibility to the extensive systemic, institutional, and interpersonal circumstances that affect these women.

Notes

1. The first book, *Black Masculinity in the Obama Era: Outliers of Society*, provides an in-depth examination of the current state of black males and identifies the impact of living in the era of the first black president (Hoston 2014). The second book, *Race and the Black Male Subculture: The Lives of Toby Waller*, uses the literary embodiment of Toby Waller from Alex Haley's highly acclaimed book and mini-series, *Roots*, as a historical figure to examine the effects of systemic racism and discrimination on black masculinity (Hoston 2016).

2. The black male subculture is defined as a broad term to include all black men. The term does not imply that black men are a monolithic or homogeneous group. One of the primary goals of each book is to contend against the narrative that black pathology is embedded within the black male subculture. The beneficiaries of white empowerment, who work to uphold the authoritative nature and structure of their supremacy, employ the notion that black men suffer from a pathology that makes them hypermasculine, violent, and criminal. This age-old lie has been planted into the mental psyche of the American people.

3. See Swaine, J., Laughland, O., Lartey, J., and C. McCarthy. 2015. "Young black men killed by US police at highest rate in year of 1,134 deaths." *TheGuardian.com*. Available at: https://www.theguardian.com/us-news/2015/dec/31/the-counted-police-killings-2015-young-black-men (December 31).

4. The city of Chicago was given this description by local rap artists such as King Louie and the news media. The number of murders in the city over the last decade has been comparable to *Operation Iraqi Freedom* (OIF). OIF started on March 20, 2003, and ended December 15, 2011, recording a total of 4,422 casualties. In that same time frame, Chicago recorded just fewer than 4200 murders.

5. This murder total is more than New York and Los Angeles combined. Both are larger cities than Chicago. New York ranks number one, and Los Angeles ranks number two. The city of Chicago is third.

6. See Gallardo, M., and L. Podesta. 2017. "762 murdered in Chicago in 2016, CPD releases plan to curb violence." *ABC7Chicago.com*. Available at: http://abc7chicago.com/news/762-murdered-in-chicago-in-2016/1681356 (January 1). It should be mentioned that 781 murders were recorded for the year. However, the CPD statistics do not include murders on the expressway, police-involved murders, self-defense murders, and murders under investigation.

7. In *Black Masculinity in the Obama Era: Outliers of Society* there is a chapter titled, "We All Came From a Woman: Rap Music and Misogyny," which discussed the misogynistic message of sexual assault and rape in rap music.

8. In a Twitter post (2015, November 14) black transgender woman, Laverne Cox (@Lavernecox), provided her own interpretation of the constructs. She wrote in response to one of her followers, "Actually its (sic) cisnormative heteronormative imperialist white supremacist capitalist patriarchy my spin on @bellhooks." Available at: https://twitter.com/lavernecox/status/665595357288640513.

9. It should be noted that black feminist scholar, Moya Bailey, coined the term "misogynoir" to describe how facets of both racism and anti-blackness alter the misogynistic experiences of black women from white women.

10. See Edwards, B. 2015. "At least 5 black women have died in police custody in July; WTF?!" *TheRoot.com*. Available at: http://www.theroot.com/articles/news/2015/07/at_least_5_black_women_have_died_in_police_custody_in_july_wtf.html (July 30).

11. See Larimer, S. 2016. "Disgraced ex-cop Daniel Holtzclaw sentenced to 263 years for on-duty rapes, sexual assaults." *WashingtonPost.com*. Available at: https://www.washingtonpost.com/news/post-nation/wp/2016/01/21/disgraced-ex-officer-daniel-holtzclaw-to-be-sentenced-after-sex-crimes-conviction/?utm_term=.bf7355883d1d (January 22).

12. See the 2015 Violence Policy Center (VPC) report, "When men murder women: An analysis of 2013 homicide data." Available at: http://www.vpc.org/studies/wmmw2015.pdf.

13. Ibid.

14. See Farr, S. 2016. "Police: Ex-Temple cops killed roommate because 'she would not submit.'" *Philly.com*. Available at: http://www.philly.com/philly/blogs/dncrime/Police-Ex-Temple-cops-conspired-to-murder-roommate-.html (August 2).

15. Ibid.

16. It is important to note that "cis-normativity" nor "hetero-cis-normativity" were discussed in this text. These terms imply that it is normal to be both cisgender and heterosexual. While these terms are indeed connected in all forms of hegemonic practices, yet different and distinctive, their omissions was not to conflate sexuality with gender but to stay grounded in a framework to understand toxicity toward black transgender women.

17. In 2017, Merriam-Webster dictionary confirmed that in 1923 the term "heterosexuality" was defined as "morbid sexual passion for one of the opposite sex." See @ MerriamWebster (2017, March 18). Available at: https://twitter.com/MerriamWebster/status/843278973081718785.

18. See Taylor, C. 2016. "Trump selects anti-LGBT bigot Mike Pence as vice president running mate." *OccupyDemocrats.com*. Available at: http://occupydemocrats.com/2016/07/14/trump-selects-anti-lgbt-bigot-mike-pence-vice-president-running-mate (July 14). In the U.S. Congress, Mike Pence outlined a political agenda to "Renew the American dream." The agenda is available at: http://web.archive.org/web/20010408125427/http://mikepence.com/issues.html.

19. See Mayer, J. 2017. "The danger of President Pence." *NewYorker.com*. Available at: https://www.newyorker.com/magazine/2017/10/23/the-danger-of-president-pence (October 23).

20. A full description of the 2011 report conducted by the National Gay and Lesbian Task Force and the National Center for Transgender Equality (NCTE), "Injustice at every turn: A report of the national transgender discrimination survey," can be found at: http://www.thetaskforce.org/static_html/downloads/reports/reports/ntds_full.pdf.

21. Ibid.

22. The 2011 National Transgender Discrimination Survey (NTDS) study, which was the most comprehensive at the time and the first large-scale national study of discrimination against transgender people, had approximately 6,456 participants. The 2015 study had 27,715 participants.

23. For a full report, see James, S. E., Herman, J. L., Rankin, S., Keisling, M., Mottet, L., and M. Ana. 2016. *Executive Summary of the Report of the 2015 U.S. Transgender Survey*. *Washington, DC: National Center for Transgender Equality*. Available at: http://www.transequality.org/sites/default/files/docs/USTS-Executive-Summary-FINAL.PDF.

24. Ibid.
25. For more information on the one-on-one interview with bell hooks, see the online version from *Trans-Scripts* 5 (2015). Available at: http://sites.uci.edu/transscripts/files/2014/10/2015_5_hooks_rev.pdf.
26. See Terry, D. 2015. "In the crosshairs." *Medium.com*. Available at: https://medium.com/hatewatch-blog/in-the-crosshairs-3700fbf2203d#.rwxk10nyh (June 9).
27. Ibid.
28. In 2016, former President Barack H. Obama designated a new national monument at the historic site of the Stonewall Uprising in New York City to honor the broad LGBTQIA equality movement.
29. In 2017, Andrea Jenkins was elected to the Minneapolis City Council. She spent years as a policy aide to former council members.
30. Greenfield-Sanders, T. 2016. *The trans list.* HBO Documentary. United States: Perfect Day Films.
31. LGBTTI2QQ is an acronym for "lesbian, gay, bi, transgender, transsexual, intersex, two-spirit, queer, and questioning."
32. See the 2015 National Coalition of Anti-Violence Programs (NCAVP) press release, "NCAVP mourns the death of Zella Ziona, a transgender woman of color killed in Gaithersburg, Maryland; the 22nd reported homicide of a transgender/gender nonconforming person NCAVP has responded to in 2015." Available at: http://avp.org/storage/documents/2015.10.7_ncavp_ma_zellazionamd.pdf.
33. Some official reports note 23 murders of transgender women. However, one of the victims, Jessie Hernandez, a 17-year-old Hispanic from Denver, Colorado designated as a gender non-conforming person. Jessie was shot by police officers while driving a stolen car.
34. In a 2017 report titled, "Unerased: Counting Transgender Lives," *Mic.com* estimates that from 2010 to 2016, 111 transgender and gender non-conforming individuals were murdered in the USA. Seventy-two percent were black transgender women. The report can be found at: https://mic.com/unerased.
35. See Gross, A. 2016. "The throwaways: How Detroit is becoming a flashpoint for violence against trans women." *MetroTimes.com*. Available at: http://www.metrotimes.com/detroit/seven-transgender-women-have-been-murdered-in-detroit-since-2011-the-harm-runs-far-deeper-than-the-headlines/Content?oid=2392648 (January 27).
36. Ibid.
37. See Holden, D. 2015. "Why are black transgender women getting killed in Detroit." *Buzzfeed.com*. Available at: https://www.buzzfeed.com/dominicholden/why-are-black-transgender-women-getting-killed-in-detroit?utm_term=.wmmOmoGq3G#.dynY2N7l17 (November 19).
38. Ibid.
39. A full description of the 2015 report, "Meaningful work: Transgender experiences in the sex trade," conducted by the National Center for Transgender Equality (NCTE), the Red Umbrella Project (RedUP), and Best Practices Policy Project (BPPP), can be found at: http://www.transequality.org/sites/default/files/Meaningful%20Work-Full%20Report_FINAL_3.pdf.
40. A full description of the 2011 report conducted by the National Gay and Lesbian Task Force and the National Center for Transgender Equality (NCTE), "Injustice at every turn: A look at black respondents in the national transgender discrimination survey," can be

found at: http://www.thetaskforce.org/static_html/downloads/reports/reports/ntds_black_respondents_2.pdf.

41. Before the close of 2015, Mike Honda, with the support of 26 Democratic co-sponsors, introduced House Resolution 561: Expressing support for support of transgender acceptance. The Resolution has two main objectives, which are to: (1) Recognize the systematic and structural challenges facing the transgender community and the need for action to improve safety and opportunity for transgender people; and (2) Express support for such community and allies through the LGBT Equality Caucus and Transgender Equality Task Force. The Resolution died in the Subcommittee on the Constitution and Civil Justice. Last action was on 01/15/2016.

42. See Tourjee, D. 2015. "He's not done killing her: Why so many trans women were murdered in 2015." *Broadly.Vice.com*. Available at: https://broadly.vice.com/en_us/article/hes-not-done-killing-her-why-so-many-trans-women-were-murdered-in-2015 (December 16).

43. The term "cisgender" is used to describe human beings whose assignment of sex at birth is congruent with their current gender identity. In a 2014 *Times* article titled, "This is what 'cisgender' means," it suggests that they are,

> People who use the word to describe themselves are often sending two messages: A) I'm hip to gender politics and B) I believe people are all the same when it comes to being normal and legitimate, even if their experience of gender identity is different. But there is no consensus on who should use the term or when.

Article available at: http://time.com/3636430/cisgender-definition (December 23). An offspring of "cisgender" is the emerging term "cishet." This term is used to describe a person who is both cisgender and heterosexual. Often the term is used in a derogatory fashion to refer to an individual who is critical of transgender people.

44. Harris (2011, p. 23) has a meaningful discussion on this point. She argues that heteropatriarchy shapes one of the most important rules of hegemonic masculinity: a "real man" is not a woman.

45. See Agu, C. 2016. "Toxic masculinity and preventing interpersonal violence." *Daily-Nexus.com*. Available at: http://dailynexus.com/2016-04-05/toxic-masculinity-and-preventing-interpersonal-violence (April 5).

46. Black feminist contributor, Esther Armah, in a 2016 *Ebony.com* piece titled, "Toxic masculinity matters" defined toxic masculinity as "deeply emotional, and simultaneously utterly dismissive and contemptuous of emotionality. Insecurity-laden, dominance-obsessed, fear-filled—it teaches boys and men to stand their ground, confront unapologetically and aggressively—except when it comes to intimate partner violence, and then it says, *look away, not your business*." Available at: http://www.ebony.com/news-views/toxic-masculinity#axzz4Nq2Epcmn (August 12).

47. See Browning, B. 2015. "Victim number 13: Transgender woman of color murdered in Dallas." *Advocate.com*. Available at: http://www.advocate.com/crime/2015/08/13/victim-number-13-transgender-woman-color-murdered-dallas (August 13).

48. The petition was archived because it did not meet the signature requirements. Information on the petition is available at: https://petitions.whitehouse.gov//petition/

formally-investigate-transphobic-violence-leading-rising-death-toll-transgender-women-color-us-0.

49. For an in-depth analysis of the BLM movement, see Lowery (2016) who provides an influential voice for the movement.

50. See Reynolds, B. 2015. "I was a civil rights activist in the 1960s. But it's hard for me to get behind Black Lives Matter." *WashingtonPost.com*. Available at: https://www.washingtonpost.com/posteverything/wp/2015/08/24/i-was-a-civil-rights-activist-in-the-1960s-but-its-hard-for-me-to-get-behind-black-lives-matter (August 24).

51. One-on-one interview with bell hooks, *Trans-Scripts* 5 (2015).

52. The BLM movement has declared May 19ᵗʰ #SayHerName National Day of Action. According to their Facebook page, "On this day, we are standing in solidarity with all Black women (cis and trans), girls, and femmes in efforts to shed light on the abuse that they endure under systems of anti-Black misogyny." For more information, see their link: http://sayhername.blacklivesmatter.com.

53. See Brydum, S. 2015. "Alicia Garza: Taking Black Lives Matter to another dimension." *Advocate.com*. Available at: http://www.advocate.com/40-under-40/2015/12/09/alicia-garza-taking-black-lives-matter-another-dimension (December 9).

54. See Ring, T. 2015. "Three more black trans women reported murdered." *Advocate.com*. Available at: http://www.advocate.com/transgender/2015/08/16/three-more-black-trans-women-reported-murdered (August 16).

55. Ibid.

56. Ibid.

57. For more information, visit the Black Lives Matter organization website. Available at: http://blacklivesmatter.com/guiding-principles.

58. See Steinmetz, K. 2014. "The transgender tipping point." *Time.com*. Available at: http://time.com/135480/ transgender-tipping-point (May 29).

59. See Driessen, K. 2015. "Houston Equal Rights Ordinance fails by wide margin." *Chron.com*. Available at: http://www.chron.com/politics/election/local/article/HERO-results-6608562.php (November 4).

60. Newport, F., and G. J. Gates. 2015. "San Francisco metro area ranks highest in LGBT percentage." *Gallup.com*. Available at: http://www.gallup.com/poll/182051/san-francisco-metro-area-ranks-highest-lgbt-percentage.aspx?utm_source=Social%20Issues&utm_medium=newsfeed&utm_campaign=tiles (March 20).

61. Annise D. Parker, Personal interview, December 7, 2015, Houston, Texas.

References

Barnard, I. 2004. *Queer race: Cultural interventions in the racial politics of queer theory*. New York: Peter Lang.

Bey, M. 2017. The trans*-ness of blackness, the blackness of trans*-ness. *Transgender Studies Quarterly* 4(2): 275–295.

Black, M. C., Basile, K. C., Breiding, M. J., Smith, S. G., Walters, M. L., Merrick, M. T., Chen, J., and M. R. Stevens. 2011. *The National Intimate Partner and Sexual Violence Survey (NISVS): 2010 Summary Report*. Atlanta, GA: National Center for Injury Prevention and Control, Centers for Disease Control and Prevention.

Cohen, C. 1999. *The boundaries of blackness: AIDS and the breakdown of black politics*. Chicago: University of Chicago Press.

Collins, P. H. 2004. *Black sexual politics: African Americans, gender, and the new racism*. New York: Routledge.

Crenshaw, K. 1989. Demarginalizing the intersection of race and sex: A black feminist critique of antidiscrimination doctrine, feminist theory, and antiracist politics. *University of Chicago Legal Forum* 1(8): 139–167.

Harris, A. P. 2000. Gender, violence, race, and criminal justice. *Stanford Law Review* 52(4): 777–807.

Harris, A. P. 2011. Heteropatriarchy kills: Challenging gender violence in a prison nation. *Washington University Journal of Law & Policy* 37(1/3): 13–65.

hooks, b. 2004. *The will to change: Men, masculinity, and love*. New York: Washington Square Press.

Hoston, W. T. 2014. *Black masculinity in the Obama era: Outliers of society*. New York: Palgrave Macmillan.

Hoston, W. T. 2016. *Race and the black male subculture: The lives of Toby Waller*. New York: Palgrave Macmillan.

Kitzinger, C. 2005. Heteronormativity in action: Reproducing the heterosexual nuclear family in after-hours medical calls. *Social Problems* 52(4): 477–498.

Kupers, T. A. 2005. Toxic masculinity as a barrier to mental health treatment in prison. *Journal of Clinical Psychology* 61(6): 713–724.

Lowery, W. 2016. *They can't kill us all: Ferguson, Baltimore, and a new era in America's racial justice movement*. New York: Little, Brown and Company.

Meyer, D. 2008. Interpreting and experiencing anti-queer violence: Race, class and gender differences among LGBT hate crime victims. *Race, Gender & Class* 15(3–4): 262–282.

Meyer, D. 2010. Evaluating the severity of hate-motivated violence: Intersectional differences among LGBT hate crime victims. *Sociology* 44(5): 980–995.

Namaste, V. 2000. *Invisible lives: The erasure of transsexual and transgendered people*. Chicago: University of Chicago Press.

Patton, M. Q. 2002. *Qualitative research and evaluation methods, 3rd Edition.* Thousand Oaks, CA: Sage.

Richardson, M. U. 2003. No more secrets, no more lies: African American history and compulsory heterosexuality. *Journal of Women's History* 15(3): 63–76.

Shugrue dos Santos, C. 2012. A community-based approach to LGBTQH IPV: One size does not fit all. *Domestic Violence Report* 18(1): 1–14.

Ware, S. M. 2017. All power to all people? Black LGBTTI2QQ activism, remembrance, and archiving in Toronto. *Transgender Studies Quarterly* 4(2): 170–180.

· 2 ·

THE BLACK TRANS IDENTITY

I miss Nikki. She had finally committed 100% to being a trans woman. She had finally said, "This is who I am!" It's just so sad because not even a year after coming out she committed suicide because her [black] cis boyfriend didn't fully accept her.

—Sophie Rush

In the wee hours of the morning on February 15, 2011, Nikki Gorgeous, a twenty-six-year-old black transgender woman from Houston, Texas, committed suicide in her apartment. The night before, Nikki and her black cisgender boyfriend were on a double-date celebrating Valentine's Day. As told by Sophie Rush, the oldest of the black transgender women featured in this book and a part of the accompanying couple, "It was a wonderful night. Everyone was having a good time." After the couples had dinner at an upscale restaurant, they proceeded to a local bar to have martinis. According to Sophie:

> Everyone was having a good time. Then a couple of [black] cis boys who were with their dates began to say some really demeaning things to us. They called us "shemales," "trannies," "chicks with dicks," all sorts of stuff. They called our male friends "gay," "faggots," "cocksuckers," etc. As someone who has been out [transitioned] for a long time, I ignored it and suggested we leave. We left and went to another spot. I thought all was forgotten. Later that night, we all parted ways. Nikki and her man went to her place. Two days later I found out she had taken a bunch of pills to commit suicide.

As the story goes, Nikki's boyfriend was quite disturbed by the egregious name-calling at the local bar. He was embarrassed that other black men called his masculinity into question in a public setting. Later that night Nikki's boyfriend violently raped her, beat her up, and then left her apartment. Not long after he left, she took a deadly cocktail of prescription pills. Nikki's body was discovered a day later by a family member.

The narrative of the actions leading to Nikki's suicide as told by Sophie exemplifies one of the many tragic circumstances that black transgender women are often faced with when attempting to establish domestic relationships with cisgender men. More importantly, this scenario singles out the most substantive theme that emerged among the black transgender women interviewed in this book, which is that destructive forms of patriarchy that persist within the black community result in a kind of toxic masculinity making these women vulnerable to the behaviors and actions of black cisgender men.

This chapter attempts to offer an expanded cultural perspective of the lived experiences of black transgender women, and explores both their gender identity and their ability and willingness to fit, or not fit, into mainstream black communal life. Because these women reject the patriarchal frame within the black community that seeks to situate them in a biological box based on their medically sex assigned at birth, it is important to analyze the multifaceted layers of their existence that is often stigmatized and frowned upon by those within the community who exhibit anti-trans attitudes and behaviors. Their sense of identity within the black community stands as the assemblage of the social constructions of race and gender identity, socioeconomic status, and a biased communal perception influenced by the ideological indicators of religion, morality, and ethics, which all have an adverse effect on their cultural acceptance.

Considered a homogenous group led and influenced by the cultural repertoires of the black church, over time the black community has slowly become more accepting of black LGBTQIA people, including black lesbian women and black gay men of all sexual variations, and of black transgender men. However, the masses of those within the black community remain defiant in their acceptance of black transgender women. These women have yet to fit within the patriarchal social structure that has defined the fabric of the black community.

Nikki Gorgeous was a black transgender woman. Through her story and others within this book, the goal is to provide an operational context for what it means to be a black transgender woman within the black community and in the larger American society. What is the societal and cultural impact of the black male-to-black female transition (MtF) on black masculinity and black femininity? What are black cisgender attitudes toward black transgender women? These questions are important to address the cultural conflicts within the black community that exists between black transgender people and blocs of black cisgender people who exhibit such anti-trans attitudes and behaviors.

Defining the "Transgender" Identity

In general, transgender is "an umbrella term that refers to all identities or practices that cross over, cut across, move between, or otherwise queer socially constructed sex/gender boundaries" (Stryker 1994, p. 251).[1] Ryan and Futterman (1997), in their study on lesbian and gay youth, describe transgender people as individuals who exhibit gender non-conforming identities and behaviors. Scholars of transgender research, across the different academic disciplines, have employed a broad spectrum of nontraditional gender expressions to define transgender people, including but not limited to, transsexuals, cross-dressers, drag kings and queens, gender queers, gender-benders, masculine women, feminine men, butch lesbian trans, and androgens (see Bornstein 1994; Bullough and Bullough 1998; Burgess 1999; Lev 2004; Bilodeau 2005; Bilodeau and Renn 2005; Coleman et al. 2012; Rossiter 2016).[2] Therefore, the term transgender encompasses all human beings who are gender-variant, including those who have transitioned or in the process of transitioning.[3]

Transgender people have an internal, psychological sense of belief that their sex assigned at birth is not congruent to their gender identity (Bullough 2000; Lev 2004; Stone Fish and Harvey 2005). Despite the broad spectrum of gender-variance, transgender people have primarily been studied in two realms: First, human beings medically assigned the sex of female at birth who have a sense of gender identity as male, female-to-male (FtM), categorized as transgender males. Conversely, human beings medically assigned the sex of male at birth who have a sense of gender identity as female, male-to-female (MtF), are categorized as transgender females. Some scholars and practitioners have argued that both exist in a dormant physical median if they do not choose sexual reassignment surgery (SRS) to complete the full physical transition. Yet, what these onlookers fail to realize from the interview data collected, is that both transgender men and transgender women live in an emotional and psychological state that allows them to transition to their gender identity and act out their gender in opposition to the heteronormative thinking that is tied to a strict gender binary in American society.

bell hooks in a 2015 interview with *Trans-Scripts* expounds on the importance of shedding the heteronormative thinking tied to a strict gender binary :

> I think people are not relating to the body [anymore] in the same way [as 20 years ago]. The body is not the litmus test. This is why transgender and transsexual issues have become so important because it centers on your critical way of being in the world, and not just your body and what you do with it.[4]

Laverne Cox, who is a transgender actress and LGBTQIA activist, in a 2014 *Huffington Post* interview parallels the thoughts of hooks when explaining how the construct of heteronormativity leads people to focus on the physical being and genitalia of transgender people and not the societal and cultural issues and concerns most affecting them. She argued in the interview:

> The preoccupation with transition with surgery objectifies trans people and then we don't get to really deal with the real lived experiences. The reality of trans people's lives is that so often we're targets of violence. We experience discrimination disproportionately to the rest of the [LGBTQIA] community … [B]y focusing on bodies, we don't focus on the lived realities of that oppression and that discrimination.[5]

To improve our comprehension of the gender identity and lived experiences of transgender people, it is critical to develop a better understanding of who these human beings are and the descriptive language and practices that define their way of life. The hope is that it will foster a comfortable societal climate to enable more transgender acceptance and inclusion in the USA without the problematic frames of patriarchy and heteronormativity clouding individuals' judgment. Such a societal climate would facilitate gender diversity and equality, use descriptive language to acknowledge gender identity, recognize their new name, and move toward gender affirmation, which are all vital in empowering an individual after they have transitioned.

Locating and Recognizing the Transgender Community

In 2016, the *Williams Institute* estimated that 1.4 million transgender people were identified to exist in the USA.[6] When controlling for racial trends in growth, 12% identified as African-American or black.[7] For several reasons, locating and recognizing members of the transgender population has been an arduous task throughout the decades.[8] First, there is the ability to ascribe to different aspects of being gender-variant and the proclivity to be considered gender non-conforming as mentioned above. Therefore, the U.S. Census and other official records kept by governmental agencies have a difficult time reporting the population size based on gender identity (see Meerwijk and Sevelius 2017).

Second, there is significant conservative legislative resistance to the idea of enacting trans-friendly federal and state laws such as transgender-inclusive nondiscriminatory measures. In 2015 anti-LGBTQIA lawmakers in Republican-led state legislatures and local municipalities around the country introduced a significant number of measures targeting and further victimizing the LGBTQIA community. At least 125 anti-LGBTQIA measures were introduced during this year at the state level; approximately 21 bills targeted transgender people. Most of the transgender measures focused on anti-trans rights in public restrooms, locker rooms, and gender-affirming health care.[9] While none of the bills were enacted, the anti-transgender legislation signifies a conservative push for such measures. Despite transgender-inclusive nondiscriminatory measures receiving the most support at the local level, legislative challenges at the state level have forced the repeal of some city ordinances, while others lost a partisan and moral war at the ballot box.

In the earlier part of 2016, the *Human Rights Campaign*[10] reported that nearly 16 state legislatures either pre-filed[11] or introduced an onslaught of anti-transgender bills ranging from public restrooms, locker rooms, gender-affirming health care to making it impossible to change the gender marker on their birth certificate.[12] The most infamous anti-transgender legislation was enacted on March 23, 2016, in the state of North Carolina. On this day, former Republican North Carolina Governor Pat McCrory and the State General Assembly enacted House Bill 2: Public Facilities Privacy & Security Act, which restricted the rights of transgender people in the state to use public bathrooms, as well as, prohibiting local municipalities from passing transgender-inclusive nondiscriminatory measures.[13] This law was introduced in response to a nondiscrimination ordinance in Charlotte that banned LGBTQIA discrimination and allowed transgender people to use the public bathroom of their preferred choice. While other states and local municipalities had progressively introduced inclusive nondiscriminatory measures to grant such rights, most of which lost at the ballot box, the adoption of this transgender-inclusive city ordinance had set a new national precedent.

Repealing this Charlotte ordinance incited a statewide civil liberties battle. Taylor et al. (2014), in their study of transgender-inclusive ordinances, indicate that the local political culture matters in relation to the state political culture in the statewide acceptance of such measures. As a result of the passage of this ordinance, the Republican-led General Assembly called a special session to craft a well-insulated discriminatory measure that preempted the liberal-leaning Charlotte ordinance. Not only did the law repeal the ordinance, but it as well, prevented other local municipalities in North Carolina from passing their own inclusive nondiscriminatory measures.

Former Charlotte mayor, Jennifer Roberts, said of the conservative backlash regarding the ordinance:

> I have to confess. I did not see this coming. What Charlotte voted on, and talked about for over a year during the campaign and in the community, was really making sure the LGBT community felt equal, felt included, and felt they would be treated equally in all aspects of our community.[14]

After its passage, LGBTQIA activists deemed House Bill 2 as the most anti-LGBTQIA bill in the country. The backlash even led some to retitle it to "Hate 2." The most severe counterattack of the bill was how it affected the economy in North Carolina. The state lost prominent entertainment and sporting events and potential incoming jobs, which significantly impacted the economy by losing out on tens of millions of dollars. An Associated Press analysis projected that House Bill 2 could have cost the state more than $3.76 billion over the next decade.[15]

In November 2016, the Democrats gained the gubernatorial seat with incoming Democratic Governor, Roy Cooper. In a political move to restore the spiraling down economy, outgoing Governor McCrory with the support of Cooper brokered a tentative legislative deal to repeal House Bill 2.[16] However, in December during a special legislative session to repeal the bill, Republican legislators at the last minute opposed such efforts. The repeal ultimately failed because Republicans sought a moratorium of six months that would prohibit local municipalities from reintroducing similar ordinances. After some months had passed, lawmakers finally reached a compromise to repeal a large part of House Bill 2. The new deal prohibits local municipalities from passing anti-discrimination ordinances until 2020.

The state of North Carolina now stands as a case study of the divisiveness in the political arena on anti-trans-related legislation and policies. Furthermore, it shows how Republicans, who controlled legislatures in 32 states at the beginning of 2016, would exercise political and legislative power during the Trump presidential era.

Third and last, only within recent years, with the celebration of the transgender lives of Janet Mock, Laverne Cox, Jazz Jennings, Caitlyn Jenner, and others through mainstream media has there been an increased willingness of transgender people to self-identify and be counted.[17] *Rolling Stone* named 2014 the "Biggest Year in Transgender History," listing the unprecedented level of transgender presence in television, music, film, and fashion.[18] In the same year, *Time Magazine* did a feature titled, "The Transgender Tipping Point: America's next civil rights frontier," to discuss the plight of transgender rights.[19]

The icing on the proverbial cake came when former President Barack H. Obama, who influenced the passage of substantive LGBTQIA measures during his presidency, referenced the term "transgender" in his 2015 State of the Union speech.[20] Obama emphatically stated that it was important to "condemn the persecution of women, or religious minorities, or people who are lesbian, gay, bisexual, or transgender. We do these things not only because they're right, but because they make us safer."[21] Janet Mock, a black transgender woman who is an author, MSNBC host, and leading voice in the transgender community, applauded his speech and articulated that, "The President's acknowledgment helps shatter the cloak of invisibility that has plagued trans people and forced many to suffer in silence."[22]

For these reasons, locating and recognizing transgender people for inclusiveness in American society has been an arduous task. However, as American society celebrates the "Biggest Year in Transgender History" and a period in history defined as "The Transgender Tipping Point," it is fundamentally vital to eliminate the status of invisibility that has afflicted many transgender lives. Creating a societal and cultural space for acceptance and inclusion is paramount, and as will be discussed throughout this book, is important to combat the systemic, institutional, and interpersonal practices against transgender people.

The Difference Between Sex and Gender

The terms of "sex" and "gender" are interwoven in the identity of human beings. Hamilton (2008), whose research argues that the terms are not equivalent, indicates that "sex" is a biological distinction, whereas, "gender" is a socially constructed phenomenon. These components of identity formation have received an abundance of attention from scholars in the different social science fields.[23]

West and Zimmerman's (1987) theory of "doing gender" supports the idea of gender as a socially constructed term. In their analysis, the authors argue against gender being an expression of natural difference. They contend that gender is not the makeup of an individual or the role an individual takes on, but instead, gender is exhibited through an individual's interactions. The notion of "doing gender" relegates us to the expectations of how American society deems that it is appropriate for men and women to behave in set ways, further reinforcing gender norms and behaviors. West and Zimmerman conclude, as well as other scholars (Martin 2004; Risman 2004; Poggio 2006), that, "An understanding of how gender is produced in social situations will afford clarification of the interactional scaffolding of social structure and the social control processes that sustain it" (p. 147).

The use of the terms "sex" and "gender" interchangeably without properly defining their meaning has greatly contributed to a unitary mindset that lumps human beings in the traditional binary of male and female. The conflation of these two components of identity formation has signified a gendered culture that, as shown, has diminished the significance of the self-variation for members of the LGBTQIA community.

The Failure of Traditional Binary Thinking

Historically, in American society, we have viewed gender options in the traditional binary of male and female. Because we live in a society where gender is embedded in our individual, interactional, and institutional dimensions, the concept of "gender" exists as a social structure that strongly defines identities, roles, appearances, and characteristics (Risman 2004). According to Stryker (2008, p. 13), gender identity is described as a "subjective sense of fit with a particular gender category." To move beyond a binary frame of reference that places transgender people in gender-specific typological categories, it is imperative to understand that gender identities and roles can be fluid, which allows them to reject such failed binaries. Existing binaries that adhere to gender norms are fundamentally flawed. Sophie Rush explained this flaw when discussing her past struggle to present herself as a man:

> I presented myself for years as a man to the outside world. As a man, society defined my role [in the household]. At the time, I was helping to take care of my family. I got up in the morning, put on my clothes, and went to work. I would have expressed my yearning to live as a woman earlier if society would have made me feel like it was "ok" to do so. Instead, I hid it. I was stealth. I was afraid to be called a "punk". Either

you are a "man" or a "punk" in the black community. Not a "man" or "woman", but a "man" or "punk".

To this day, my family wants my gender identity to be that of a man. I'm not a "gender bender." I don't have a "mixed gender." My gender [identity] is that of a woman. I missed out on some good years of my life because society told me I needed to present myself as a man.

To provide a comparative point of view, Jessica Sugar, who is black and Filipino, expounded that even in the Philippines gender roles are clearly defined, however, transgender people are making strides:

In the Philippines, gender roles are strictly defined. Boys take after their fathers. Girls take after their mothers. That is tradition. This is why I was surprised when I saw a trans woman being voted into public office.[24] That is very surprising.

Wilchins (2002), who points out the inherent flaw of this binary thinking, articulates that, "Gender is a system of meanings and symbols—and the rules, privileges, and punishments pertaining to their use—for power and sexuality: masculinity and femininity, strength and vulnerability, action and passivity, dominance and weakness. One can see in it the outlines of something that links misogyny, homophobia, transphobia, and the restricted way we raise our youth" (pp. 25–26). The important work of Wilchins helps to further reveal we live in a typologically driven society where the gender identification of a human being is often assumed or found to be true by the following questions: Are you a male or a female? Are you masculine or feminine? For most, the answer to these heteronormative questions fostered in a patriarchal culture is multifaceted. There is no causation between the concepts of male and masculinity nor female and femininity. Is masculinity what males do? Is femininity what females do? Or, are these merely artificial constructs? The alignment with such artificial constructs support gendered social structures to facilitate comfortability for those who possess anti-trans attitudes and behaviors.

In the same work, Wilchins asks, "What is it about binaries that so captivates our thinking: Men/women, gay/straight, M-to-F/F-to-M, white/black, real/artificial, male/female, lesbian/feminist" (p. 46)? Jae Palmer, 20 years old, who once identified as a black transgender woman but detransitioned to his previous sexual orientation as a black gay man, accounted for this question in his response by stating, "Folks have always tried to put me in a box all my life. It doesn't work. They wanted me to choose a gender identity. They wanted me to choose a sexual orientation. But I can identity whatever way I feel. That is the beauty of life. Right now, I am a [black] gay man. That is my [sexual] orientation and [gender] identity."

The heteronormative force field in American society made to protect its gendered social structures has failed in many ways. Coyote and Spoon (2014), in their collection of autobiographical essays, lyrics, and images, present the argument that both of them have failed at their attempt to fit into the traditional gender binary. Both authors were medically assigned female at birth but have gone through their entire life identifying along the LGBTQIA continuum. Because none of the labels adequately applied to their identity as human beings, the authors have decided to retire from fitting into a gender category (or sexual orientation) altogether. It is their belief that no sexual orientation or gender identity fits their human reality. Coyote writes:

> My friends call me he, or they. The government and most of my family call me she. The media calls me she, because I don't trust them enough to request that they do anything else. My lovers call me sweetheart. Or baby. Somewhere in all of that I find myself. These are all, after all, only words. (p. 224)

From the perspectives of Coyote and Spoon, concentrating on a traditional gender binary rather than welcoming the sexual orientation or gender identity of each human being and moving beyond this binary vision further widens the standing of gender inequality in the USA.

The Gender Norm of Appearance

There is a continual challenge to gender norms that take full shape in the physical appearance and presentation of transgender people. Because "doing gender" is often defined by appearance and presentation, transgender men and transgender women are often faced with a myriad of decisions regarding how they would like to present themselves to the world. In some cases, transgender people are led to believe due to societal and gender norms that only two options are available to them. They are either to make the life decision whether to both simulate their chosen gender identity and learn the customary attributes associated with that identity to be passable, or live in a state of mental being where the psychological transition outweighs the physical transition.

The majority of transgender people transition toward normative genders to present themselves as "passable" to avoid societal and cultural rejection (Stieglitz 2010; MacDonald 2013). In a 2015 *Advocate* article, the well-used term in the transgender community of "passable" refers to "being perceived as cisgender while presenting as one's authentic gender identity."[25] For instance, a transgender man is likely to dress in perceived masculine attire, whereas, a transgender woman will dress in perceived feminine attire in an attempt to send a distinct gender message in their appearance. According to Mia Ryan, 29 years old, one of the participants interviewed:

> There is a very big emphasis placed on appearance as it pertains to transitioning … Many people assume that individuals, like myself, have transitioned for much longer because I am considered "passable." I have a feminine voice, I carry myself like a lady, and my body type is similar to a cisgender woman. I can't lie being viewed as "passable" has been a benefit.

On the other hand, transgender people who are not considered "passable" as a cisgender person are constantly vulnerable to harassment, discrimination, abuse, and violence (Namaste 2000; Lombardi et al. 2002). The benefit of passing as a cisgender person lowers their probability of experiencing these forms of victimization. Venus Love, who is 31 years old, expressed that transgender people who are not considered "passable" have a tough time on a daily basis. She compared passability related to transgender men and women:

> Trans men have to maintain a masculine demeanor at all times. If not, a cis man will want to fight him. If they do [maintain a masculine demeanor], a cis man may still want to fight him to show his dominance over the trans man. These trans men can't win, especially around black people. [Black] cis men will try them (i.e., want to fight). And even though [black] trans men are more accepted than us by [black] cis men, another reason they have to watch themselves is that one of their friends, who is a [black] cis man, will get drunk or high one night and try to rape them. They still have a vagina and bleed every month.
>
> On the other hand, if trans women are not "passable," they will hear "tranny," "she-male," and other insulting shit all day. The crazy part is, if you are passable, [black] cis men will feel betrayed, deceived, or even embarrassed when attracted to you. When they find out you are a trans woman, the situation may become violent.

Passing as a cisgender person can provide a psychological and social advantage to transgender people. It is a part of the normalization process and one of the privileges that helps to insulate transgender people (Sycamore 2006). Mia Ryan also indicated that:

> The journey of transitioning physically is the most challenging. I say that because most trans individuals transition mentally long before they began transitioning

physically. I won't say life is easier for a trans person who is "passable" but as you begin to live life as a transgender person and figure out how to become confortable in your skin, the ability to blend in helps.

In contrast, when transgender people attempt to be "passable," it can be seen as an erasure of their transgender identity (Davy 2011). Jae Palmer elaborated on this stance by explaining his decision to detransition:

> Part of the reason I decided to detransition, for lack of a better word, back to gay male is that I received so much criticism as a trans woman from other trans women. Because I was "passable," these other [trans] women would give me hell because they were not. It's a lot of jealousy in the trans community. Some circles applauded me for looking cis, other circles wanted me to maintain some male features so that it was known that I was a trans woman and not a "deceiver," "pretender," or "fake." The shit was confusing as hell.

The degree to which a small subset of the women in the transgender community feel that the pursuit of "passability" is a form of erasure which follows a hyper-feminine social script and supports the traditional gender binary, should be accepted as legitimate (Serano 2007). However, Sophie Rush, who describes her experience of experimenting with different feminine looks over the years, said in defense of attempting to "pass" articulated, "It took me a long time to be comfortable with my outward appearance. I don't agree that it takes away from who I am to try to identify as a cis woman. You can't identify as a woman looking like a man. That's the God's honest truth."

Hello Black Religious Community, I'm Black Trans

For the black community, there is a strict heteropatriarchal way of experiencing the perception of gender, which is grossly shaped by the ideological indicators of religion, morality, and ethics. For most in this communal setting, "doing gender" comes with a hierarchical order of God, man, and woman. Challenging this gender hierarchy is often deemed blasphemous and ungodly. According to the teachings of the black church, the phrase from the Bible (Genesis 1:27), "God created mankind in His own image," is argued to have framed the image of God as a male and set the gender hierarchy of civilization. Equally important, this established a set of unwritten conservative gender ideologies that have worked to uphold distinctive gender roles in the church that limits women's authority and active role. Such patriarchal thinking extends to black LGBTQIA people who fall below black women in the hierarchical order.

A Houston-based black pastor, who agreed to be interviewed on the condition of anonymity about his opinion of the increasing visibility of black transgender people within the black community, explained:

> I am at a loss for words. The devil is really working overtime. First, it was the coming out of gays and lesbians. Now it is the confused men in dresses trying to pass as women and the girls dressed like men. God birthed man to be the head of the household. God birthed woman to be his companion and submissive. The gender order is set. These new gender identities being created jeopardize the foundation of how God saw the world. No earthly man or woman can contest that. What these [transgender] people are doing is an abomination. I hope they seek God to correct their lives.[26]

The pastor spoke to the contentious and complex relationship between the black church and the black LGBTQIA community. The social institution of the black church, as well as the majority of its membership, have stood as a public face in opposition to black LGBTQIA acceptance and same-sex marriages, despite knowing that a large base of its congregation are lesbian and gay. Lincoln and Mamiya (1990), in their analysis of the black church in the African-American experience, find that black churches hold an influential position within the black culture. In many ways, the heads of these black churches symbolically represent the voice of the patriarchal ideology that sets a heteronormative foundation. This foundation is the blueprint for the rituals, daily practices, and overt messages broadcast in the black church, which relays that heterosexuality is the societal, cultural, and gender norm.

In their biblical imagery and language, these churches foster homophobic attitudes and behaviors. Religious-driven homophobia reverberates from the mouths of ministers, pastors, bishops, and reverends, which is reinforced from scriptures within the Bible.[27] In many of their minds, they have become sexual and gender overseers ordained by God who uses the same biblical methods of oppression against black LGBTQIA people that were employed during slavery to maintain a gender hierarchy. Pitt (2010), in his analysis of anti-gay religious messages, found that black LGBTQIA people absorb the sting of the churches' negative messages by neutralizing the moral authority of the churches' messengers.

From their bully pulpits, the heads of these black churches speak out against the black LGBTQIA community even with some of them linked to scandal. For example, in 2010, the late Bishop Eddie Long, an anti-gay preacher, was accused of sexually abusing four young men in his youth ministry.[28] He, along with others in the black church, have preached the black gospel but engage in affairs, appoint lesbians and gays to leadership positions in the church, and each Sunday rejoice from the sounds of the choir that are usually filled with lesbian and gay members.

This is the type of hypocrisy that has forced the majority of black LGBTQIA churchgoers to live in the closet. C. Riley Snorton (2014) in his important book, *Nobody Is Supposed To Know*, explains that black LGBTQIA people are often forced to live on the down low, a form of self-regulation that requires a conspicuous silence. In his analysis, Snorton investigates the role that the black church plays as a symbol of sexual scrutiny. Dowshen et al. (2011, p. 411), in their study of religiosity as a protective factor against HIV, write that, "[M]any LGBT youth feel isolated from religious institutions whose beliefs are in conflict with their gender or sexual identity." However, while the black church speaks out passionately against this group, most black lesbian women, black gay men, black bisexual men and women, and even some black transgender men, fill the congregation on Sundays more than black transgender women. According to the black pastor interviewed:

> The [black transgender women] people who want to be women do not come to my church as often as others. I know there are people of all sexual orientations [in the church]. I am not naïve to that. But those people [black transgender women] rarely come. The older women in the congregation try to convince them [black transgender women] to come to God (i.e., become saved) each time one of them does come to church to deliver them from their demonic ways. These people are feeding into a system that destroys the image of the black man. They should read Matthew 19:5–6.[29]
> Matthew 19:5–6: King James Version (KJV)

5: And said, For this cause shall a man leave father and mother, and shall cleave to his wife: and they twain shall be one flesh?

6: Wherefore they are no more twain, but one flesh. What therefore God hath joined together, let not man put asunder.

Even the Honorable Minister Louis Farrakhan from the Nation of Islam (NOI), a black religious leader best known for organizing the 1995 Million Man March to build black male consciousness, voiced a similar position in a 2016 interview with the Breakfast Club morning show by saying, "[T]he black male *is* being feminized!"[30] This proclamation was made in agreement with one of the co-hosts, Charlamagne Tha God, who said, "It's almost like if they [white America] can't kill us [black men], they want to feminize us."[31] Farrakhan's shortsighted thinking to blame a larger societal construct speaks to the grand, and largely understood reality within the black community, that the greater majority of black cisgender religious leaders will not concede to accepting that black gay men and black transgender women have embraced their sexual orientation and gender identity, which deconstructs their perceived gender norms. Such leaders believe that systemic and institutional factors have worked to emasculate and feminize the black man. This thinking is established by the grand ideas of a gender hierarchy and belief system in the black cultural realm that oppresses feminine traits in men who they believe should exhibit constructed masculine traits.

In her seminal book that centers on black AIDS victims, *The Boundaries of Blackness*, Cohen (1999) moves beyond the traditional paradigm of studying whiteness in relation to the dominant group's oppression of the marginalized group, to a hierarchical structure of the marginalized groups' method of oppressing members within the group. She identifies the social institution of the black church as the antagonist who failed to take action to help black AIDS victims within the black community. The extension of her argument is that black church leaders neglect issues such as AIDS because these issues are "cross-cutting" which "affect only certain segments of a marginal group" (p. 13).

In the leadership position, the heads of black churches practice a form of secondary marginalization, which employs "rhetoric of blame and punishment—directing it at the most vulnerable and stigmatized [within a community]" (p. 27). This form of marginalization ostracizes members of the black community who the church believes to behave outside of the normative rules and cast as individuals with moral failings. One of the ways Cohen discusses secondary marginalization is in the context of gay and lesbian sexualities. She argues that the black communities' acceptance of divergent sexualities is incumbent upon how they interpret the intersectionality of their gay and lesbian existence. Inasmuch, the black church serves as the negotiator to parishioners in the acceptance and inclusion of different sexualities.

Applying the framework of Cohen to black transgender women, secondary marginalization facilitates a culture that allows cisgender blacks within the community and culture to push their conservative gender ideologies and norms onto the backs of these women. As an outcome, the black church can perceive the gender identity of black transgender women as a mere moral failing and the issue of their deaths as "cross-cutting" brought on due to their sinful life choice to transition from their medically assigned sex. Their attempt to distance themselves from this issue contributes largely to the crisis of black transgender deaths being ignored within the black community.

The come-to-Jesus-moment for the social institution of the black church is occurring in the twenty-first century as more black transgender people are willing to attend the black church and force this social institution to face them transitioning and/or coming out to the black community and to speak out against transphobic violence and murders. Graham (2014), in his exploratory study of black transgender women navigating their way in different community institutions, indicates that "[Black transgender women] paradoxically found faith to be both an internal source of strength or resilience, as well as others' moral rationale for transphobia and discrimination" (p. 281). One participant, Arianna Gray, the youngest of the black transgender women at 19-years-old and a college student at a predominantly white institution who goes to church every Sunday, explains, "I grew up in the church. I won't stop going to church. I am a child of God. He made me in his own image. No man or woman's voice in a church is greater than the voice of God. I actually came out in the church. I showed up one Sunday and presented myself to God [and the church] as a transgender woman."

Beyond question, the lens of the social institution of the black church through which most black cisgender people view black LGBTQIA people has lost its devout strength. The manipulation of Bible scriptures to rebuke black LGBTQIA people and their lives, cast them as sinners, manufacture phobias, and hinder acceptance has shown itself to be a religious failure. In the past, the black church coupled with the activist energy of the black community had by and large worked hand in hand to fight for the equal rights, protections, and individuality of its members.

Today, some of the heads of these black churches do not equate the fight against the historical discrimination of black people to the "tiny minority group" of black LGBTQIA people, especially black transgender people.[32] In 2016, Rev. Bill Owens, the president of the Coalition of African-American Pastors (CAAP), in opposition to former President Barack H. Obama advocating for single-sex bathrooms said, "Transgendered persons are not asking for equal rights—they are asking for special rights that violate the privacy of women and simple common sense."[33] Rev. Owens goes on to expound that:

> Black Pastors will not allow the homosexual and transgender community to rob Black Americans of their battle for civil rights!
>
> If the [Dr.]Rev. Martin Luther King were alive to see this today, he would be angered in the same way that Jesus was angered when he turned over the tables of the money changers.[34]

The culture of socially conservative attitudes within the black church values masculinity over femininity and is afraid to alleviate secondary marginalization and accept any sexual orientation and gender identity that is counter to the doctrine in the Bible. This, in turn, leads some of its most devoted members to live double lives by "Standing on the word of God" on Sundays and having to "Keep it on the down low" Monday through Saturday. Having said that, no black LGBTQIA group is more affected by the continuation of conservative gender ideologies than black transgender women. According to Mia Ryan, "I watch church from my couch. This way I won't be judged while I'm trying to praise the Lord. The church members don't love me … I tried to attend church, but they shunned me … I love God. He is the only one who can judge me."

The Black Transgender Juxtaposition

Within the black transgender juxtaposition, transgender men and transgender women are viewed as similar in their decision to choose a gender identity in line with their psychological sense of belief but each receive different treatment among members within the black community. Woven throughout both of their lives is the idea of them facing comparable cultural issues and concerns. According to the black transgender women interviewed about the cultural incompetence of the black community, they outlined three concerns that separated the two transgender groups: (1) The transitioning and/or coming out period, (2) The benefiting of masculine privilege and acceptance gained by black transgender men, and (3) The lack of black solidarity within the black community following transgender deaths.

Transitioning and/or Coming Out Period

Transitioning and/or coming out for transgender people to the black community requires more cultural understanding than coming out as lesbian, gay, or the acknowledgement of bisexuality. While the terms are sometimes used interchangeably, "transitioning" refers to the period when an individual changes from expressing their gender beyond their private life, which can include changing one's name, gender marker, gender appearance and mannerisms, and SRS (Lombardi and Davis 2006). The act of "transitioning" and/or "coming out" is an important process in the acceptance of one's gender identity or sexual orientation and the willingness to share with the outside world (see e.g., Gagne et al. 1997; Morrow 2006; Hunter 2007; Koken et al. 2009; Zimman 2009; Beemyn and Rankin 2011; Nemoto et al. 2011; Graham et al. 2014).

Gagne et al. (1997) indicate that the societal backlash of coming out as a transgender person can evoke emotions ranging from stress, frustration, lack of self-control, to suicide. In a later study, Beemyn and Rankin (2011), who analyze the psychological toll placed on transgender people who live in secrecy prior to coming out to the public as a new gender identity, find that the fear of harassment and discrimination continues to loom in their decision. Nemoto et al. 2011, in their study of racial differences in social support, found that black transgender women hid their transgender identity more than all other races. This finding is consistent with Graham et al. (2014, p. 105) who found that these women "concealed their identities as a way of managing sexual and gender conformity pressure" brought on from family relationships to avoid the negative responses associated with newfound gender identity. The anticipated fear these women, of all races and ethnicities, face makes some of them more likely to live in a stealth state rather than attempt to find intrapersonal harmony.[35]

To continue from Arianna Gray's narrative of coming out in the church,

> I showed up to church as a transgender woman. Before that, everyone knew that I was a gay man although no one said anything to me about it. On that day, I got to church early and sat in the front. It was my way of introducing my new self to God.

Like her description of coming out, which speaks to the before and after of the presentation of her gender appearance and seeking of acceptance, other black transgender women interviewed talked about the time period they came out as it relates to the reception from family, friends, and other members within the black community.

According to Naomi Mars, a 25-year-old escort, who described her nuclear family as a "close family unit" until she informed them she was a "woman trapped in a man's body," explains that, "The decision to identify as a transgender woman affected my family a lot. In the beginning, I thought that coming out was a big mistake. They basically disowned me. There continues to be love there, but it's not as strong anymore." Another participant, Alexandria Sweet, a 24-year-old escort, tells that during her transition period that her family and friends had a lot of questions. For instance, they asked her:

> Are you really transgender or experimenting with cross-dressing? What does it feel like to be a woman with a penis? Are you going to take hormone pills? Are you doing the [sex reassignment] surgery? Do we have to call you "she"? Some felt it was a choice. Others felt it was just a phase.

She further stated when discussing how her family reacted to her transition:

> My father and mother really just didn't understand. They thought they'd done some-
> thing wrong as parents. My aunts thought I was confused. My uncles thought I just
> hadn't had any good pussy. But it was my grandmother who took it the hardest. She
> is a die-hard Christian. She feels like I am a sinner destined to go to Hell. She has
> completely disowned me. Everyone had an opinion about how my life was supposed
> to be. I heard from all of them, "be a man," "act like a man," and "you're setting a bad
> example for your younger brothers and sister."

The reaction from Naomi and Alexandria's family corroborates the findings of Gagne et al. (1997) and Willoughby et al. (2008) who both suggest that acceptance by parents makes the process easier, whereas, on the other hand, disapproval can have an adverse effect on their life decisions. Alexandria was adamant that, "If my family had accepted me, maybe I wouldn't have turned to the streets."

The patriarchal stronghold of the black community expects black cisgen-der men who have not fallen victim to negative structural and culture forces to gradually enter manhood and become the head of the household. This normative idea about the gender hierarchy is compromised by the notion that men should be "the dominant" and women should be "the subservient." This is predicated by the belief that the man should be assigned the position of head of household, which is birthed in the ideological womb of the conserva-tive Christian church (see Ephesians 5:22–24, KJV) who believes heteronor-mative thinking is the foundation of fundamental Christian values.

bell hooks (2004b), in her book, *We Real Cool*, explains that during slav-ery free and enslaved black men were taught patriarchal masculinity based on Christian values:

> They had to be taught that it was acceptable to use violence to establish patriarchal
> power. The gender politics of slavery and white-supremacist domination of free black
> men was the school where black men from different African tribes, with different lan-
> guages and value systems, learned in the "new world," patriarchal masculinity. (p. 2)[36]

Hunter and Davis (1992, p. 472), in their article that explores the meaning of black manhood, contend that patriarchal gender norms of manhood within the black community is constructed from the competing interests of "family role expectations grounded in patriarchy and the comparatively egalitarian work and family roles in Afro-American families." Thus, black cisgender men, who are privileged by the gender hierarchy, are influenced and molded by normative ideas about gender.

The black community holds black cisgender men to a dangerous standard of demonstrating masculine norms in ways that collocate feminine norms. Venus Love provided her perspective of masculinity by stating:

> The older generation sees black men as the head of the household who have been through a lot in their lives to provide for their families. Some older black women have told me that I am disrespecting the legacy of the black man and even the black woman. They tell me I need to be a man and act like a man.

Venus went on to further discuss her upbringing by affirming:

> I can understand both positions. When I was young, I was told [by my mom] to be a strong black man, finish school, get a good job, and start a family with a beautiful black wife. Based on the history of black men [being absent and going to jail], my mother laid out those goals for me. She wanted me to be a successful black man and start a family. I'm still trying to get her to understand that gender roles have changed over time. Most black males are in prison so most black homes don't have established [gender] roles. There is no man of the house anymore.

Bobbie Golden, 27 years old, in her response parallels the emotions of most of the participants when family and friends are not accepting of their transition. She explained:

> When the family support was not there, that is when shit went south for me. In my mind, I thought if my family wouldn't support me, then no one would support me. When I tried to get a job as a trans, they would throw my application in the trash before I left the interview. That's what initially led me to this lifestyle [of being an escort]. No family support and no job. To make the shit worse, my mother told me I belonged on the streets with the trash. With me now working as an escort, she was right. It's exactly where I landed, too. It hurts knowing that my mother thinks that I'm a piece of trash. That's why I decided to take college courses. I want to eventually change my life.

Black transgender women interviewed were adamant that the patriarchal family structure dominants the thinking within the black community. They believed that one of the black family's worse nightmares is to witness their child, who was medically assigned male at birth and is supposed to represent the embodiment of masculinity and lineage, dressed in women's clothing. Alexandria Sweet described how her father cried each and every time he saw her after she first transitioned. She explained that, "My father cried like a baby. I'm the oldest. I'm a junior. We look just alike. We'll we used to. So when he saw me as a trans woman, he took it hard. Really hard."

Due to the fact that sexual orientation and gender identity are topics that are not heavily discussed inside of the black nuclear family setting and beyond, coming out as LGBTQIA within the black community is often met with resistance. For black transgender people, especially black transgender women, such resistance can come with a cost. This cost can be severe due to the fixed masculine script as to how it is perceived that black men should act and sexually behave (Stephens and Phillips 2003) making heterosexuality the most accepted sexuality and established gender identity.

The Benefiting of Masculine Privilege

Within the black community, black transgender men often receive more cultural acceptance than black transgender women. The apparent cultural distinction of their degree of acceptance is attributed to the patriarchal frame within the black community that allows some black members to view black transgender men in a masculine way (Blackwood 2009; Abelson 2014a; Abelson 2014b). Abelson (2014b), in her research on dangerous masculine privileges, argues that a heteropatriarchal power structure allows transgender men to participate in a less privileged form of hegemonic masculinity, which is cultivated in an idealized pattern of masculinity.[37] According to Connell and Messerschmidt (2005, p. 832), "Hegemonic masculinity was understood as the pattern of practice (i.e., things done, not just a set of role expectations or an identity)." In this sense, Abelson (2014a, p. 12) contends that,

> Masculinities, as patterns of practice, can be enacted by people with various gender and sex embodiments or other aspects of social location (e.g., race, class, sexuality, ability, etc.); however, particular patterns of practice adhere more easily to some kinds of people.

This, in turn, fosters a climate for black transgender men to be more socially and culturally accepted than black transgender women maintaining a gender hierarchy.

To the accepting members of the black community, black transgender men in many respects are viewed as black cisgender men with the expectation to adopt and practice traditional masculine norms. Individuals who were once strictly subjugated to the oppressive elements of femininity have a newfound masculinity and gender privilege, which in part, redefines their masculinity and serves to normalize them in a black patriarchal culture. Thus, this gained privilege is a real and tangible element of black transgender life within the black community.[38]

Moreover, if these black transgender men possess the ability to be "passable" as cisgender men, it adds another layer of privilege to their being (Koyama 2003). And in certain cases to help further validate their newfound masculinity and gender privilege, some black transgender men and black studs have adopted a practice that extends beyond an exterior masculine appear where they wear dildos (also known as "straps") as a genitalia accessory underneath their clothing. Marco Gregory, a 22-year-old black transgender man[39] from Houston, Texas, gives credibility to this practice by confirming that, "This validates the manhood of some black trans and studs. It gives them a dick print and makes them feel like a real nigga."[40] This masculine ideology rests on the idea that male genitalia are correlated to masculinity. These black transgender men and black studs seek to prove their manhood and this is an internal part of their masculine sexuality and identity.

According to Naomi Mars, in her opinion of the black community's acceptance of black transgender men, argues "they have it better than us":

> First of all, black trans men can float back and forth from Stud [lesbian] to trans. They don't have to assume the negative label of "trans". That actually goes for all trans men not just the black ones. But the black trans men blend in well in the black community. The ones who keep up their appearance, keep a fresh fade (haircut), and wear fly clothes. They look like men, talk with a swagger, and have a bunch of Lipsticks [lesbians] running behind them. Once they get the deep voice, beard, and tattoos, some of them look exactly like some of these dudes on the street.

Naomi provides context for black transgender men who previously lived in masculinity ways prior to transitioning. She, along with the other participants, maintained that when black butch, dyke, or stud lesbians decide to transition a masculine shell of privilege is formed to serve as a cocoon for protection during the stages of doubt, indecision, and uncertainty before gaining total confidence with their decision to exist as transgender men within the black community. Lee (2009, p. 18) argues that these "[lesbians] hug the line between femininity and masculinity" in the transgender space. This self-process helps to insulate them from the "disrespectful whispers," "shouts of public ridicule," "alienation," and criticisms. Sophie Rush articulated this position well:

> When we change our gender appearance it's like "bam!". For black trans men, most of them looked like or tried to look like men before the transition. They have less explaining to do. But we have to disregard our emotions and feelings and explain to the very people who are disrespecting the fuck out of us why we should be able to express our gender identity. If that isn't a form of privilege that trans men are granted, then I'll be damned.

The newfound masculinity and gender privilege of black transgender men does not totally shield them from violence and murder within the black community. These social constructs merely make available more opportunities for them to escape some of the victimizations that exist in the realm of femininity. Marco Gregory maintained,

> The world is not peaches and cream for us either. We get our share of bullshit. The police fuck with us. Black niggas will fuck with us sometimes, too. Some will fuck with me [e.g., harassing, bullying], but others will say "man, that's a chick, chill out." But I can agree that we don't catch hell like trans women. Them bitches get it the worse.[41]

In comparison, black transgender women do not enjoy the same lasting gender privilege. Arguably being medically assigned the sex of male has allotted these women an unearned benefit, even if short-lived, of living within a hegemonic masculine integument. However, after their transition, there is no newly founded privilege, but rather, they are individuals who are deemed more of a societal and cultural target. Their feminine appearance eradicates them of their masculine privilege and exposes them to the oppressive elements of both black masculinity and black femininity fueled by anti-trans attitudes and behaviors directed toward them.

While male privilege is not a monolithic power granted to black transgender men within the black community, their gender appearance does allow a more advantageous position—even if it is a privileged victim status. Thus, for black transgender men there is a sort of liberation that they experience within the black community that empowers them, and at the same time, it highlights the multiple intersections of marginalization faced by black cisgender women and black transgender women, one gender group who has never experienced privilege and the other who has leveraged their privilege to be whole with their true gender identity. For black transgender women, this unfortunately, pushes them to the lowest on the human totem pole within the black community.

The Lack of Black Solidarity

Within the broader context of black lives, another urgent cultural concern from black transgender women is that the BLM movement has not responded with the same level of activism to transgender deaths as white police-involved deaths of unarmed black men. Inasmuch, their deaths have not led to collective action to promote a sense of solidarity to address this growing epidemic. According to Bledsoe et al. (1995, p. 435), "[blacks] with a greater sense of solidarity are more likely to see themselves as personal victims of discrimination,

to perceive widespread discrimination against blacks as a group." Alexandria
Sweet explained that, "there's no solidarity among black people like some
would think." She went on to express:

> They keep shouting "Black Lives Matter," but we all know they're not talking about
> us. They're not allies for black trans. Our lives should matter just as much as any
> black person.

Her response introduced the belief that the solidarity within the black
community that encouraged the BLM movement does not fully extend to
black transgender women.

As a whole, the black transgender women interviewed were disappointed
in the lack of support in addressing transphobic violence and murders. They
expected that the BLM movement would energize activism within the black
community, regardless of ideological beliefs, to advocate on their behalf due to
the overwhelming number black transgender women murdered. Alexandria
added:

> We need a group like the "Check It" in D. C. to band together against these phobic
> motherfuckers.[42] I get it all day. I'm harassed at the grocery store, Wal-mart, even
> Popeyes. A bitch can't even sit down to eat her chicken. Either these niggas talk shit,
> try to fight me, try to fuck me, or mean absolutely no good. Most of the time, I really
> don't know what to expect. But what I do know is that these Black Lives Matter
> people ain't doin' shit to help protect me.

Within the black community, transgender activists have had to work to
build solidarity to address these issues and concerns. The number of black
transgender women being murdered in the USA is rising and vast attention to
this epidemic hides behind the minimal political and legislative influence of
the BLM movement. Venus Love, in her assessment of the black community
speaking out against the victimization of black transgender women by black
cisgender men, declared:

> The black community doesn't care about us. Do they march in the streets when we
> are murdered? Hell no. Do they protest day and night like in Ferguson? Hell no.
> There's no love for us honey. Our lives don't matter. You know why? The reason is
> because it's our so-called brothers doing the killing. They ain't my fuckin' brothers!

Alexandria further stated in her opinion of the BLM movement:

> I bet if I take off this wig and say a white police officer shot me, them Black Lives
> Matter folks would come to the rescue then. They're hypocrites. If you care about

THE BLACK TRANS IDENTITY

black people so much, then care about all of us. Since I chose a life they don't agree with, my life doesn't matter as much as the next black person. That's wrong and everyone knows it.

The other participant's opinions of the BLM movement were in line with Alexandria and Venus. They believed that the black community and the BLM movement has a rank and file approach when addressing cultural issues and concerns, which begins with racialized state violence against black cisgender men and black cisgender women and ends with intra-racial violence among black people.

Black Cisgender Attitudes Toward Black Transgender People

The critiques of the black community and the BLM movement by black transgender women note an unending ideological trend within a community that does not, as a whole, accept their ability to be gender non-conforming. The problem that this point dramatizes is the consistent negative attitudes toward black transgender women by black cisgender members of their own community. In this section, the goal is to analyze black cisgender attitudes toward black transgender women. To date, there has been very little research conducted on public attitudes toward transgender people (Tee and Hegarty 2006; Norton and Herek 2013; Flores 2015).[43]

In the most recent study, Flores (2015), in his study of attitudes toward transgender rights, provided two important findings: First, cisgender people who were more informed about transgender people had more supportive attitudes. Second, cisgender people who previously had interpersonal contact with lesbian and gay people led to a secondary transfer of positive attitudes. On the other hand, Norton and Herek (2013) in their study of heterosexuals' attitudes toward transgender people, found that attitudes toward transgender people were more negative among heterosexual men than women. Such negative attitudes were associated with the acceptance of a rigid gender binary, higher level of psychological authoritarianism, political conservatism, anti-egalitarianism, and religiosity. Most notably in their research was that "attitudes toward transgender people were significantly more negative than attitudes toward sexual minorities" (p. 749).

To gauge black cisgender attitudes toward black transgender women, I surveyed the attitudes of a convenience, nonprobability sample of blacks in the greater Houston, Texas metropolitan area (see Appendix A.2). In an ideal world, this analysis would include a random sample that contains a cross-city comparison in order to make the findings more generalizable. However, the liberal-leaning climate of the city of Houston who had an openly lesbian mayor, Annise D. Parker, from 2010 to 2016, and ranks among the top metropolitan cities with a large LGBTQIA population, makes this social environment a suitable research laboratory to provide a baseline of data for studying cisgender attitudes toward LGBTQIA people.[44]

Descriptive Results

In the survey, the attitudes of black cisgender people toward black LGBTQIA people and black transgender people were analyzed to identity variations among the respondents' attitudes. The response pattern varied among the respondents when viewing LGBTQIA people as a whole and then a subset of transgender people. More than half of the respondents positively agreed that the black community should be accepting of black LGBTQIA people and black transgender people. Black cisgender women revealed more positive attitudes than black cisgender men. In contrast, the respondents presented negative attitudes when asked should the black community view black transgender women the same way we view black cisgender women.

Overall, 97% of the respondents indicated that they had come into contact with a black LGBTQIA person, but only 8% reported that they had come in contact with a black transgender person. The gap in this finding presumes that it is potentially attributed to the refusal of transgender people to transition outwardly within the black community and live as stealth, which lessens their presence. Six percent of the respondents had come in contact with a black transgender woman and a mere 2% with a black transgender man.

In Table 2.1 where the respondents were asked, "Do you agree that the black church should condemn black LGBTQIA people?" the majority of the respondents disagreed (strongly 46%, somewhat 15%). This finding singled a departure from the strong homophobic attitudes fostered in the black church. Conversely, a third of the respondents agreed (strongly 30%, somewhat 4%) that the black church should condemn black LGBTQIA people and not be affirming of their sexual orientation and gender identity. The negative attitudes of this pool of respondents showed that the black church's religious beliefs toward black LGBTQIA people continues to have an influence on some members of the congregation.

Table 2.1. Black Cisgender Attitudes toward Black LGBTQIA People.

Items	Strongly disagree (5)	Somewhat disagree (4)	Neutral (3)	Somewhat agree (2)	Strongly agree (1)	Response Mean
Do you agree that the black church should condemn black LGBTQIA people?	46% (129)	15% (42)	4% (12)	4% (12)	30% (84)	3.43
					Total N = 279	

Note: The values of this question are in the reverse to coincide with the direction of the opinions of the respondents for Tables 2.2 and Table 2.3.

In Table 2.2 when the respondents were asked do they agree that the combination of religious, moral, and ethical beliefs inhibit black Americans from accepting black LGBTQIA people, an overwhelming majority agreed (strongly 62%, somewhat 15%). Despite agreeing that ideological signifiers inhibit acceptance, two-thirds of the respondents positively agreed (strongly 49%, somewhat 18%) that the black community should be accepting of black LGBTQIA people (see Table 2.2). When controlling for gender, the majority of black cisgender women surveyed (90%) agreed that the black community should be accepting of black LGBTQIA people (63% strongly agreed, 27% somewhat agreed).

Table 2.3 shows that ideological signifiers as well weighted heavily when answering questions related to black transgender people. A large majority of the respondents agreed (strongly 85%, somewhat 8%) that the combination of religious, moral, and ethical beliefs inhibit black Americans from accepting black transgender people. When the respondents were asked, "Do you agree that the black community should be accepting of black transgender people?" results were mixed as more than half agreed (strongly 32%, somewhat 22%). A third of the respondents disagreed (strongly 26%, somewhat 11%) and 9% were neutral (see Table 2.3). Within this finding, again, black cisgender women showed the most acceptance. When controlling for gender, the majority of black cisgender women surveyed (80%) agreed that the black

Table 2.2. Black Cisgender Attitudes toward Black LGBTQIA People.

Items	Strongly agree (5)	Somewhat agree (4)	Neutral (3)	Somewhat disagree (2)	Strongly disagree (1)	Response Mean
1. Do you agree that the combination of religious, moral, and ethical beliefs inhibit black Americans from accepting black LGBTQIA people?	62% (173)	15% (41)	3% (8)	14% (39)	6% (18)	4.12
2. Do you agree that the black community should be accepting of black LGBTQIA people?	49% (136)	18% (51)	1% (3)	6% (16)	26% (73)	3.58
					Total N = 279	

community should be accepting of black transgender people (50% strongly agreed, 30% somewhat agreed).

In Table 2.3 negative attitudes toward black transgender people were most prevalent when the respondents were asked, "Do you agree that the black community should view black transgender women the same way we view black cisgender women?" Seventy-five percent of the respondents strongly disagreed and 16% somewhat disagreed (see Table 2.3). This finding suggests that in spite of more than half of the respondents' acceptance of black transgender people, they do not agree that black transgender women should be viewed the same way as black cisgender women.

Predictive Model Results

Table 2.4 assesses the importance of variables in predicting black cisgender acceptance using ordinary least squares regression models. The table is divided into two models. This analysis confirms that black cisgender women were more accepting of both black LGBTQIA people and black transgender

Table 2.3. Black Cisgender Attitudes toward Black Transgender People.

Items	Strongly agree (5)	Somewhat agree (4)	Neutral (3)	Somewhat disagree (2)	Strongly disagree (1)	Response Mean
1. Do you agree that the combination of religious, moral, and ethical beliefs inhibit black Americans from accepting black transgender people?	85% (237)	8% (22)	0% (1)	5% (15)	2% (4)	4.70
2. Do you agree that the black community should be accepting of black transgender people?	32% (89)	22% (62)	9% (25)	11% (30)	26% (73)	3.23
3. Do you agree that the black community should view black transgender women the same way we view black cisgender women?	2% (5)	3% (8)	4% (11)	16% (46)	75% (209)	1.40
						Total N = 279

people than black cisgender men. Moreover, it shows that favorable attitudes were best predicted when black cisgender people did not believe that the ideal of religion was most influential in their daily lives.

In line with the descriptive results, black cisgender women had more favorable attitudes than black cisgender men. In both models, the variable of gender was statistically significant and in the predicted direction. This finding assumes that the negative attitudes of black cisgender men ultimately points to the heteronormative thinking toward black LGBTQIA people and black transgender people to secure their own predisposed masculinity (see Herek and Capitanio 1995; Lemelle and Battle 2004). Interesting in the findings is that in spite of the variations of black LGBTQIA people such as gay men and transgender women who stand in competition with black cisgender women

58 TOXIC SILENCE

Table 2.4. OLS Models Predicting Black Cisgender Acceptance.

Independent Variables	Model 1 Black LGBTQIA	Model 2 Black Transgender
Religion	.43**	.31**
	(.19)	(.09)
Contact	−.76	−.23
	(.49)	(.08)
Gender	−.37*	−.29*
	(.12)	(.08)
Education	−.33	−.20
	(.10)	(.06)
Income	.22	.15
	(.07)	(.03)
Age	−.18	−.12
	(.05)	(.04)
Constant	.41	.32
N	279	279
R2	.22	.17

$*p < .05. **p < .01. ***p < .001.$

for the limited pool of available black cisgender men in the USA, measuring their acceptance did not render negative results.

The measure of religion is based on the question, "How important is the ideal of religion in your life today?" Again, in both models the variable of religion was statistically significant and in the predicted direction (see Table 2.4). Black cisgender people who were somewhat less religious in their daily lives held favorable attitudes toward acceptance. In comparison, and as expected, those whom the ideal of religion played an integral role in their daily lives would have more negative attitudes. As previously talked about, black cisgender people who believe that the black church is a monolithic group led by a singular ideological voice would shun the notion of accepting a sexual orientation or gender identity outside of the traditional gender norm. This overlaps with the descriptive analysis that found that the majority of the respondents disagreed the black church should condemn black LGBTQIA people.

To gauge more completely the negative attitudes toward black transgender people within the black community, Tables 2.5 and 2.6 asked the respondents about their perceptions of black transgender men and black transgender women. While the response rate was low for these particular questions, the

Table 2.5. Black Cisgender Perceptions of Black Transgender Men.

Respondents	What is your perception of black transgender men?
1.	Cool I guess.
2.	It's hard to describe. I don't really know any but I know lesbians that look like men.
3.	Girls that dress like men.
4.	I'm confused to the whole thing honestly.
5.	My sister is a stud that likes women. Cool with me.
6.	To each its own. Not my cup of tea.
7.	Why dress like a man and date women? I don't get it.
8.	No comment. It's stupid to me.
9.	I'm all right with it.

responses themselves provide more narrative context for the positive and negative attitudes about black transgender people. Reading the responses to Table 2.5, it shows that the respondents were more likely to express relatively positive attitudes toward black transgender men. For example, the responses ranged from, "Cool I guess" to "Girls that dress like men" to "I'm confused to the whole thing honestly" (see Table 2.5). Table 2.6 reveals a difference in perception as the respondents were more likely to express negative attitudes toward black transgender women. For example, the responses ranged from, "Gross!" to "Why lord why" to "God save them" to "They need to be in someone's church" to "I have a friend that is trans" to "The world is coming to an end" to "Be a man like God created you" (see Table 2.6). These negative attitudes further highlight that certain cisgender members within the black community hold strong anti-trans attitudes.

Conclusion

This chapter has looked at the societal and cultural acceptance and inclusion of black transgender women. Within the black community, their gender identity is confronted by the perils of a black patriarchal culture. In the struggle for societal and cultural acceptance, perhaps the two most significant extractions from the findings were: First, black cisgender women were more accepting of black LGBTQIA people and black transgender women than black cisgender men. This finding is molded within the heteronormative thinking that leads black cisgender men to adhere to a fixed hegemonic masculinity that under

Table 2.6. Black Cisgender Perceptions of Black Transgender Women.

Respondents	What is your perception of black transgender women?
1.	Gross!
2.	Why lord why.
3.	God save them.
4.	These are not real women.
5.	Chicks with dicks.
6.	Perverts.
7.	They really should be ashamed of themselves.
8.	Everyone wants to be different now a days.
9.	I feel sorry for them. I pray God will deliver them.
10.	Black Trans Lives Matter.
11.	They are disgusting.
12.	We are always hurting us. Be a man.
13.	They need to be in someone's church.
14.	WTF!
15.	Sick individuals. Stay away from me.
16.	God bless them.
17.	Stop trying to trick men. It's a trap.
18.	They are confused.
19.	My uncle dressed like a woman. He died of AIDS.
20.	I love all people. We are all created equal.
21.	You mean I have to compete with men in dresses, too? I'll never be able to find a good black man.
22.	Some black men really need help.
23.	I kind of get it. But then again I don't.
24.	They scare me.
25.	I have a friend that is trans. Cool person.
26.	The world is coming to an end.
27.	No father in the home.
28.	A couple of them go to my school. I don't see a problem with them.
29.	I don't understand to be quite honest.
30.	No Comment.
31.	WTF!
32.	They nasty.
33.	Be a man like God created you.

no circumstances can be challenged in ways that feminize the exterior of their existence. Second, which is not favorable to black transgender women, is that black cisgender people viewed them as a false equivalent to black cisgender women. This finding leads to the assumption that their presence is conditionally accepted until it interferes with the traditional gender norm of what constitutes a black cisgender woman.

In a March 10, 2017 news broadcast with UK's Channel 4 discussing the inclusion of transgender women into the larger feminist movement, popular African author and feminist, Chimamanda Ngozi Adichie, who has become a leading voice on feminist issues, argued that transgender women have an intersectional privilege that makes it difficult to see them as cisgender women. The interviewer asked her a series of questions and Adichie's response sparked controversy:

> Does it matter how you arrived at being a woman? I mean, for example, if you are a trans woman who grew up identifying as a man, who grew up enjoying the privileges of being man? Does that take away from becoming a woman? Are you any less of a real woman?[45]

She answered these questions by replying:

> When people talk about, 'are trans women, women' my feeling is that trans women are trans women. I think if you've lived in the world as a man with the privileges that the world accords to men, and then sort of changed, switched gender, it's difficult for me to accept that then we can equate your experience with the experience of a woman who has lived from the beginning in the world as a woman, and who has not been accorded those privileges that men are.[46]

Adichie's comments sparked rage from the transgender community who believed she appropriated the identity of transgender women in the space of feminist progress. By separating transgender women from cisgender women, opponents of her comments insisted that Adichie inferred that transgender women have less of a claim to womanhood because of structural privileged experiences. On the same day of the broadcast, transgender activist, Raquel Willis, in a series of Twitter responses countered the comments:

> We know exactly what you mean when you say, "Trans women are trans women," but can't simply say, "trans women are women."[47]

> Cis women don't need to feel threatened by trans womanhood. If your experience means less because trans women exist, that's your problem.[48]

When you ostracize and devalue trans women and their womanhood, you are operating as a tool of the patriarchy.[49]

Adichie and others feminists who have voiced this similar opinion publicly, have been accused of enabling transphobic rhetoric when excluding transgender women from "womanhood" on the basis of "sex." Days later in a lengthy Facebook post Adichie attempted to clarify her earlier comments, but did not retract them:

> A trans woman is a person born male and a person who, before transitioning, was treated as male by the world. Which means that they experienced the privileges that the world accords men. This does not dismiss the pain of gender confusion or the difficult complexities of how they felt living in bodies not their own.
>
> Because the truth about societal privilege is that it isn't about how you feel. (Anti-racist white people still benefit from race privilege in the United States). It is about how the world treats you, about the subtle and not so subtle things that you internalize and absorb.
>
> This is not to say that trans women did not undergo difficulties as boys. But they did not undergo those particular difficulties specific to being born female, and this matters because those experiences shape how adult women born female interact with the world.[50]

The use of this assembled information strongly indicates that the intersectionality of race, gender identity, socioeconomic status, and the biased communal perception of transgender women within the black community continues to objectify the community itself as a narrowly cast cultural environment that adheres to normative ideas about gender and sexuality.

The fact is, such findings pose an important question: Is the black community deeply committed to fostering an inclusive environment for black transgender women? While there is a rising tide of public awareness about black transgender people who have emerged from the shadows within the black community, from the present findings the immediate answer is an emphatic "No." This makes the ideal of community a tenuous concept for black transgender women in the relationship between acceptance and tolerance. Herek (1990, p. 328) argues that, "People who transgress gender roles remain at the low end of the hierarchy of acceptability."

Moving forward, non-acceptance of black transgender women within the black community raises the most severe cultural concern, which is that factions of black cisgender people disregard their internal, psychological sense of belief that their sex assigned at birth is not congruent to their gender identity and purely observe them as individuals who have chosen to participate in a destructive human act. This rationale has provoked the impulse for some to view black transgender women as collateral black bodies, which as a result, has exposed them to transphobic violence and murders. To this end, Chapter 3 utilizes an intersectional approach that provides situational and cultural contexts to comprehend further the types of violence affecting black transgender women, which is essential in the urgent need to preserve their humanity.

Notes

1. In 2012, *The Diagnostic and Statistical Manual of Mental Disorders* (DSM-5: 302.85) made the decision to no longer classify individuals who are gender non-conforming or transgender as a mental disorder. In this edition of the DSM, the term "gender identity disorder," which was used to diagnose transgender individuals was officially changed to "gender dysphoria," to describe the emotional distress that can result from "a marked incongruence between one's experienced/expressed gender and assigned gender."

2. In 1910, Dr. Magnus Hirschfield (1868–1935) coined the word "transvestite" in his book, *The transvestites: An investigation of the erotic drive to cross dress.* He is known as the "Einstein of Sex." Harry Benjamin, M. D. (1885–1986) made popular the term "transsexual" when he disagreed with sexologist David O. Cauldwell's (1897–1959) claim that transsexual people were mentally unfit. See Benjamin's (1954) piece, "Transsexualism and transvestism as psychosomatic and somatopsychic syndromes." *American Journal of Psychotherapy* 8(2): 291–230.

3. It should be noted that gender identity continues to be an ever-evolving entity that encompasses a multitude of contemporary terms.

4. For more information, see *Trans-Scripts 5* (2015) titled, "Conjuring *Ain't I a Woman*: An interview with bell hooks." Available at: http://sites.uci.edu/transscripts/files/2014/10/2015_5_hooks_rev.pdf.

5. See Tannehill, B. 2014. "The fatal transgender double standard." *HuffingtonPost.com.* Available at: http://www.huffingtonpost.com/brynn-tannehill/the-fatal-transgender-dou_b_4571932.html (January 10).

6. See Flores, A. R., Herman, J. L., Gates, G. J., and T. N. T. Brown. 2016. "How many adults identify as transgender in the United States?" *The Williams Institute.* Available at: http://williamsinstitute.law.ucla.edu/wp-content/uploads/How-Many-Adults-Identify-as-Transgender-in-the-United-States.pdf.

7. See Flores, A. R., Brown, T. N. T., and J. L. Herman. 2016. "Race and ethnicity of adults who identify as transgender in the United States." *The Williams Institute.* Available at: http://williamsinstitute.law.ucla.edu/wp-content/uploads/Race-and-Ethnicity-of-Transgender-Identified-Adults-in-the-US.pdf.

8. In 2017, the U.S. Census Bureau indicated that it would not include questions regarding sexual orientation and gender identity for the 2020 U.S. Census. No previous U.S. Census has ever included LGBTQIA people.

9. See Luk, S. 2016. "New report shows rise in anti-transgender legislation in 2016." *GLAAD.org.* Available at: http://www.glaad.org/blog/new-report-shows-rise-anti-transgender-legislation-2016 (February 23).

10. See the 2016 Human Rights Campaign (HRC) report, "Anti-transgender legislation spreads nationwide, bills targeting transgender children surge." Available at: http://hrc-assets.s3-website-us-east-1.amazonaws.com//files/assets/resources/HRC-Anti-Trans-Issue-Brief-FINAL-REV2.pdf.

11. The act of pre-filing a bill is done prior to the beginning of the legislative session. Such bills are assigned a number and made available to the general public prior to the first day of session. Bills are introduced and read on the first day of the session having the full 90 days to be considered for passage.

12. Transgender activists have speculated that state legislatures introduced gender marker bills to prohibit a trickle-down effect of societal and cultural acceptance. In many cases, recognizing transgender people based on the ability for them to change their gender marker varies from state to state. One example is that many states require proof of SRS as a prerequisite to recognize transgender identity and to change one's gender marker. As a result of this prerequisite, most transgender people will elect not to attempt to change their birth given names and gender marker with the social security administration office. Instead, these transgender people, in most cases transgender women, will assume a pseudonym. For more information, see the 2015 American Civil Liberties Union (ACLU) report, "Transgender people and the law." Available at: https://www.aclu.org/sites/default/files/field_pdf_file/lgbttransbrochurelaw2015electronic.pdf.

13. The bill is officially titled, "An Act to Provide for Single-sex Multiple Occupancy Bathroom and Changing Facilities in Schools and Public Agencies and to Create Statewide Consistency in Regulation of Employment and Public Accommodations." Available at: http://www.ncleg.net/Sessions/2015E2/Bills/House/PDF/H2v0.pdf.

14. See Lang, N. 2016. "Charlotte mayor on HB2 backlash: 'I did not see this coming.'" Advocate.com. Available at: http://www.advocate.com/politicians/2016/5/20/charlotte-mayor-hb2-backlash-i-did-not-see-coming (May 20).

15. For more information, see the 2017 Associated Press analysis "How AP tallied the cost of North Carolina's bathroom bill." APnews.com. Available at: https://apnews.com/ec6e9845827f47e89f40f33bb7024f61/How-AP-tallied-the-cost-of-North-Carolina's-%22bathroom-bill%22 (March 27).

16. It is important to note that ahead of the special legislative session to repeal House Bill 2, the Charlotte city council in a 7–2 vote repealed the portion of the ordinance that allowed transgender people to use a public bathroom or locker room of their preferred choice.

17. A 2016 GLADD study, "Where we are on TV," found that broadcast TV has reached the highest percentage of LGBTQ series regulars. According to Sarah Kate Ellis, GLAAD president and CEO, "While it is heartening to see progress being made in LGBTQ representation on television, it's important to remember that numbers are only part of the story, and we must continue the push for more diverse and intricate portrayals of the LGBTQ community." Available at: http://www.glaad.org/files/GLAAD-2015-WWAT.pdf.

18. See Grace, L. J. 2014. "11 ways 2014 was the biggest year in transgender history." RollingStone.com. Available: http://www.rollingstone.com/culture/features/11-ways-2014-was-the-biggest-year-in-transgender-history-20141223 (December 23).

19. See Steinmetz, K. 2014. "The transgender tipping point." Time.com. Available at: http://time.com/135480/ transgender-tipping-point (May 29).

20. In unison with these remarks, in 2015, Obama appointed a transgender woman, Raffi Freedman-Gurspan, as the first openly transgender White House staff member. Freedman-Gurspan served as an outreach and recruitment director in the White House Office of Presidential Personnel.

21. See Steinmetz, K. 2015. "Why it's a big deal that Obama said 'trangender'." Time.com. Available at: http://time.com/3676881/state-of-the-union-2015-barack-obama-transgender (January 21).

22. Ibid.

23. According to J. A. Simpson and E. S. C. Weiner (1989) in the Oxford English Dictionary, one of the first known uses of the term "gender" dates back to 1387 C. E. when T. Usk wrote "No mo genders been there but masculine and femynyne, all the remnaunte been no genders but of grace, in faculte of grammar."

24. See Sawatzky, R. 2016. "Philippines elects first transgender woman to congress." *CNN. com*. Available at: http://www.cnn.com/2016/05/10/asia/philippines-transgender-geraldine-roman (May 10).

25. See Kosciesza, A. J. 2015. "Op-ed: I'm a trans man who doesn't 'pass'—and you shouldn't either." *Advocate.com*. Available at: http://www.advocate.com/commentary/2015/05/20/op-ed-im-trans-man-who-doesnt-pass-and-you-shouldnt-either (May 20).

26. Anonymous, Personal interview, February 16, 2016, Houston, Texas.

27. During slavery the same Bible was used to justify a process known as "break the buck" in which white male slave owners purchased black male slaves to fulfill their homosexual needs.

28. See Martinez, E. 2010. "Bishop Eddie Long scandal: He wanted sex in church, says accuser Jamal Parris." *CBSNews.com*. Available at: http://www.cbsnews.com/news/bishop-eddie-long-scandal-he-wanted-sex-in-church-says-accuser-jamal-parris (October 1).

29. Ibid., Anonymous, Personal interview.

30. This claim is flawed for two reasons: First, "femininity" is a social construct. Second, sexual variance has existed since the creation of human life. The whole discussion confuses both sexual orientation and gender identity. Sexual orientation denotes an individual's sexual identity, whereas, gender identity is more fundamentally tied to personal identity.

31. See The Breakfast Club (2016, May 24). *Minister Farrakhan full interview at The Breakfast Club Power 105.1* [Video file]. Available at: https://www.youtube.com/watch?v=--xe-7G4VnZE. It should be mentioned that the Breakfast Club morning show is an influential media outlet for black voices. It is an American syndicated radio show that airs in more than 15 major markets in the USA.

32. See Berry, S. 2016. "Black pastors slam Obama Admin's equivalence of gender identity ideology with black civil rights." *Breitbart.com*. Available at: http://www.breitbart.com/big-government/2016/05/13/black-pastors-slam-obama-admins-equivalence-of-gender-identity-ideology-with-black-civil-rights (May 13).

33. Ibid.

34. Ibid.

35. Koken et al. (2009) found that in some cases transgender women of color experienced verbal and physical abuse at the hands of their own family members when disclosing their transgender identity.

36. For a more comprehensive discussion of patriarchal violence during slavery, see Patterson (1998).

37. Connell (1987, 1995) provides an in-depth analysis of the concept of hegemonic masculinity.

38. See transgender men explain the validity of male privilege in a MTV Braless video (2016, August 19) titled, *Trans Men Explain Male Privilege* [Video file]. Available at: https://www.youtube.com/watch?v=0KGJS0IhSoE.

39. Anonymous, Personal interview, March 14, 2016, Houston, Texas. Although this chapter only obtained one interview from a black transgender man, a number of black transgender men and/or black stud lesbians were contacted to participate.

40. See an example from a WorldStarHipHop.com video (2016, September 23) titled, "She's pissed: Stud pulls out her strap on after being told she doesn't have [a] real penis!—"I'm a real n*gga." [Video file]. Available at: http://www.worldstarhiphop.com/videos/video.php?v=wshhv56907j0H97V37k4.

41. Ibid., Anonymous, Personal interview.

42. The 'Check It' is a black all-LGBT gang in Washington, DC whose mission is to protect themselves from forms of racist, homophobic, and transmisogynist violence.

43. See Herek and Capitanio (1995) for a similar discussion on black heterosexuals' attitudes toward lesbians and gays in the USA.

44. See Newport, F., and G. J. Gates. 2015. "San Francisco metro area ranks highest in LGBT percentage." *Gallup.com*. Available at: http://www.gallup.com/poll/182051/san-francisco-metro-area-ranks-highest-lgbt-percentage.aspx?utm_source=Social%20Issues&utm_medium=newsfeed&utm_campaign=tiles (March 20).

45. See Channel 4 News (2017, March 11). *Chimamanda Ngozi Adichie Interview* [Video file]. Available at: https://www.youtube.com/watch?v=KP1C7VXUfZQ.

46. Ibid.

47. See @RaquelWillis_ (2017, March 10). Available at: https://twitter.com/RaquelWillis_/status/840370359396311040.

48. See @RaquelWillis_ (2017, March 10). Available at: https://twitter.com/RaquelWillis_/status/840370598924582912.

49. See @RaquelWillis_ (2017, March 10). Available at: https://twitter.com/RaquelWillis_/status/840370764691910656.

50. See Chimamanda Ngozi Adichie's Facebook post (2017, March 12). Available at: https://www.facebook.com/chimamandaadichie/photos/a.469824145943.278768.40389960943/10154893542340944/?type=3&theater.

References

Abelson, M. J. 2014a. *Men in context: Transmasculinities and transgender experiences in three US regions.* Unpublished doctoral dissertation. University of Oregon: Eugene, OR.

Abelson, M. J. 2014b. Dangerous Privilege: Trans men, masculinities, and changing perceptions of safety. *Sociological Forum* 29(3): 549–570.

Beemyn, G., and S. Rankin. 2011. *The lives of transgender people.* New York: Columbia University Press.

Bilodeau, B. L. 2005. Beyond the gender binary: A case study of transgender college student development at a Midwestern university. *Journal of Gay and Lesbian Issues in Education* 2(4): 29–44.

Bilodeau B. L., and K. A. Renn. 2005. Analysis of LGBT identity development models and implications for practice. *New Directions for Student Services* 2005(111): 25–39.

Blackwood, E. 2009. Trans identities and contingent masculinities: Being tombois in everyday practice. *Feminist Studies* 35(3): 454–480.

Bledsoe, T., Welch, S., Sigelman, L., and M. Combs. 1995. Residential context and racial solidarity among African-Americans. *American Journal of Political Science* 39(2): 434–458.

Bornstein, K. 1994. *Gender outlaw: On men, women, and the rest of us.* New York: Routledge.

Bullough, B., and V. L. Bullough. 1998. Transsexualism historical perspectives, 1952 to present. In D. Dallas (Ed.), *Current concepts in transgender identity* (15–34). New York: Garland Publishing.

Bullough, V. L. 2000. Transgenderism and the concept of gender. *International Journal of Transgenderism* 4(3): Available at: http://www.symposion.com/ijt/gilbert/bullough.htm (January 1, 2007).

Burgess, C. 1999. Internal and external stress factors associated with the identity development of transgendered youth. In G. P. Mallon (Ed.), *Social services with transgender youth* (35–47). Binghamton, NY: Harrington Park Press.

Cohen, C. 1999. *The boundaries of blackness: AIDS and the breakdown of black politics.* Chicago: University of Chicago Press.

Coleman, E., Bockting, W., Botzer, M., Cohen-Kettenis, P., DeCuypere, G., Feldman, J., Fraser, L., Green, J., Knudson, G., Meyer, W. J., Monstrey, S., Adler, R. K., Brown, G. R., Devor, A. H., Ehrbar, R., Ettner, R., Eyler, E., Garofalo, R., D., Karasic, H., Lev, A. I., Mayer, G., Meyer-Bahlburg, H., Hall, B. P., Pfaefflin, F., Rachlin, K., Robinson, B., Schechter, L. S., Tangpricha, V., van Trotsenburg, M., Vitale, A., Winter, S., Whittle, S., Wylie, K. R., and K. Zucker. 2012. Standards of care for the health of transsexual, transgender, and gender-non-conforming people, version 7. *International Journal of Transgenderism* 13(4): 165–232.

Connell, R. W. 1987. *Gender and power.* Sydney: Allen and Unwin.

Connell, R. W. 1995. *Masculinities.* Berkeley: University of California Press.

Connell, R. W., and J. Messerschmidt. 2005. Hegemonic masculinity: Rethinking the concept. *Gender and Society* 19(6): 829–859.

Coyote, I. E. and R. Spoon. 2014. *Gender failure.* Vancouver: Arsenal Pulp Press.

Davy, Z. 2011. *Recognizing transsexuals: Personal political and medicolegal embodiment.* London: Ashgate Publishing Group.

Dowshen, N., Young, C. F., Johnson, A. K., and R. Garofalo. 2011. Religiosity as a protective factor against HIV risk among young transgender women. *Journal of Adolescent Health* 48(4): 410–414.

Flores, A. R. 2015. Attitudes toward transgender rights: Perceived knowledge and secondary interpersonal contact. *Politics, Groups, and Identities* 3(3): 398–416.

Gagne, P., Tewksbury, R., and D. McGaughey. 1997. Coming out and crossing over: Identity formation and proclamation in a transgender community. *Gender and Society* 11(4): 478–508.

Graham, L. F. 2014. Navigating community institutions: Black transgender women's experiences in schools, the criminal justice system, and churches. *Sexuality Research and Social Policy* 11(4): 274–287.

Graham, L. F., Crissman, H. P., Tocco, J., Hughes, L. A., Snow, R. C., and M. B. Padilla. 2014. Interpersonal relationships and social support in transitioning narratives of black transgender women in Detroit. *International Journal of Transgenderism* 15(2): 100–113.

Hamilton, C. J. 2008. *Cognition and sex differences.* New York: Palgrave Macmillan.

Herek, G. M. 1990. The context of anti-gay violence: Notes on cultural and psychological heterosexism. *Journal of Interpersonal Violence* 5(3): 316–333.

Herek, G. M., and J. P. Capitanio. 1995. Black heterosexuals' attitudes toward lesbians and gay men in the United States. *The Journal of Sex Research* 32(2): 95–105.

hooks, bell. 2004b. *We real cool: Black men and masculinity.* New York: Routledge.

Hunter, S. 2007. *Coming out and disclosures: LGBT persons across the lifespan.* Binghamton: Haworth Press.

Hunter, A. G., and J. E. Davis. 1992. Constructing gender: An Exploration of Afro-American men's conceptualization of manhood. *Gender and Society* 6(3): 464–479.

Koken, J. A., Bimbi, D. S., and J. T. Parsons. 2009. Experiences of familial acceptance—Rejection among transwomen of color. *Journal of Family Psychology* 23(6): 853–860.

Koyama, E. 2003. The tranfeminist manifesto. In R. Dicker and A. Piepmeier (Eds.), *Catching a wave: Reclaiming feminism for the 21st century* (244–259). Boston: Northeastern University Press.

Lee, A. 2009. The role of butch/femme relationships in transgender activism: A codependent mutualism. *Sanford Undergraduate Research Journal* 8: 18–23.

Lemelle, A. J., and J. Battle. 2004. Black masculinity matters in attitudes toward gay males. *Journal of Homosexuality* 47(1): 39–51.

Lev, A. I. 2004. *Transgender emergence: Therapeutic guidelines for working with gender-variant people and their families.* Binghamton: The Haworth Clinical Practice Press.

Lincoln, C. E., and L. H. Mamiya. 1990. *The black church in the African-American experience.* Durham: Duke University Press.

Lombardi, E., and S. M. Davis. 2006. Transgender health issues. In D. Morrow and L. Messinger (Eds.), *Sexual orientation & gender expression in social work practice* (343–363). New York: Columbia University Press.

Lombardi, E. L., Wilchins, R. A., Priesing, D., and D. Malouf. 2002. Gender violence: Transgender experiences with violence and discrimination. *Journal of Homosexuality* 42(1): 89–101.

MacDonald, J. 2013. An autoethnography of queer transmasculine femme incoherence and the ethics of trans research. In N. K. Denzin (Ed.) *40th Anniversary of Studies in Symbolic Interaction (Studies in Symbolic Interaction, Volume 40)* (129–152). Bingley: Emerald Group Publishing Limited.

Martin, P. Y. 2004. Gender as social institution. *Social Forces* 82(4): 1249–1273.

Meerwijk, E., and J. M. Sevelius. 2017. Transgender population size in the United States: A meta-regression of population-based probability samples. *The American Journal of Public Health* 107(2): 1–8.

Morrow, D. F. 2006. Coming out as gay, lesbian, bisexual, and transgender. In D. F. Morrow and L. Messinger (Eds.), *Sexual orientation and gender expression in social work practice: Working with gay, lesbian, bisexual, and transgender People* (129–149). New York: Columbia University Press.

Namaste, V. 2000. *Invisible lives: The erasure of transsexual and transgendered people*. Chicago: University of Chicago Press.

Nemoto, T., Bodeker, B., and M. Iwamoto. 2011. Social support, exposure to violence and transphobia, and correlates of depression among male-to-female transgender women with a history of sex work. *American Journal of Public Health* 101(10): 1980–1988.

Norton, A. T., and G. M. Herek. 2013. Heterosexuals' attitudes toward transgender people: Findings from a national probability sample of U.S. adults. *Sex Roles* 68(11–12): 738–753.

Patterson, O. 1998. *Rituals of blood: Consequences of slavery in two American centuries*. New York: Basic Civitas Books.

Pitt, R. N. 2010. "Killing the messenger": Religious black gay men's neutralization of anti-gay religious messages. *Journal for the Scientific Study of Religion* 49(1): 56–72.

Poggio, B. 2006. Editorial: Outline of a theory of gender practices. *Gender, Work and & Organization* 13(3): 225–233.

Risman, B. J. 2004. Gender as a social structure: Theory wrestling with activism. *Gender & Society* 18(4): 429–450.

Rossiter, H. 2016. She's always a woman: Butch lesbian trans women in the lesbian community. *Journal of Lesbian Studies* 20(1): 87–96.

Ryan, C., and D. Futterman. 1997. Lesbian and gay youth: Care and counseling. *Adolescent Medicine* 8(2): 207–374.

Serano, J. M. 2007. *Whipping girl: A transsexual woman on sexism and the scapegoating of femininity*. Berkeley: Seal Press.

Snorton, C. R. 2014. *Nobody is supposed to know: Black sexuality on the down low*. Minneapolis: University of Minnesota.

Stephens, D. P., and L. D. Phillips. 2003. Freaks, gold diggers, divas, and dykes: The sociohistorical development of adolescent African American women's sexual scripts. *Sexuality and Culture* 7(1): 3–49.

Stieglitz, K. A. 2010. Development, risk, and resilience of transgender youth. *The Journal of the Association of Nurses in AIDS Care* 21(3): 192–206.

Stone Fish, L., and R. G. Harvey. 2005. *Nurturing queer youth: Family therapy transformed*. New York: W. W. Norton & Company.

Stryker, S. 1994. My words to Victor Frankenstein above the village of Chamounix: Performing transgender rage. *GLQ: A Journal of Lesbian and Gay Studies* 1(3): 237–254.

Stryker, S. 2008. *Transgender history*. Berkeley: Seal Press.

Sycamore, M. B. 2006. *Nobody passes: Rejecting the rules of gender and conformity*. Berkeley: Seal Press.

Taylor, J. K., Tadlock, B. L., Poggione, S. J., and B. DiSarro. 2014. Transgender-Inclusive ordinances in cities: Form of government, local politics, and vertical influences. In J. K. Taylor and D. P. Haider-Markel (Eds.), *Transgender rights and politics: Groups, issue framing, & policy adoption* (135–154). Michigan: University of Michigan Press.

Tee, N., and P. Hegarty. 2006. Predicting opposition to the civil rights of trans persons in the United Kingdom. *Journal of Community and Applied Social Psychology* 16(1): 70–80.

West, C., and D. H. Zimmerman. 1987. Doing gender. *Gender & Society* 1(2): 125–151.

Wilchins, R. 2002. A certain kind of freedom: Power and the truth of bodies—four essays on gender. In J. H. Nestle (Ed.), *Genderqueer: Voices from beyond the sexual binary* (42–44). Los Angeles: Alyson Books.

Willoughby, B. L. B., Doty, N. D., and N. M. Malik. 2008. Parental reactions to their child's sexual orientation disclosure: A family stress perspective. *Parenting: Science and Practice* 8(1): 70–91.

Zimman, L. 2009. 'The other kind of coming out': Transgender people and the coming out narrative genre. *Gender and Language* 3(1): 53–80.

· 3 ·

BLACK TRANSPHOBIC
VIOLENCE AND MURDERS

It's important to look at the intersectional piece, that we're usually talking about trans women of color, that there's something about—that black bodies are under attack in this culture, and black trans bodies are under attack. So it's important for us to remember that.

—Laverne Cox, 2014 interview with *Democracy Now!*

Papi Edwards. Lamia Beard. Tyra Underwood. Yazmin Vash Payne. In 2015, their deaths set a noticeable pattern of the growing epidemic of the murders of black transgender women in the USA. Increased attention to their deaths came on the heels of a 2014 interview with *Democracy Now!* where transgender actress and activist, Laverne Cox, declared, "black trans bodies are under attack."[1] This outcry from a notable voice in the transgender community became more of a reality as black transgender women accounted for more than three-fourths of total deaths in the following year.

Papi Edwards, 20 years old, died from a single gunshot to the chest on January 9, 2015. According to a 2015 *Buzzfeed* article, "Papi got shot because she was a transgender female," said a witness named Tiffany and a close friend of Edwards who witnessed the shooting.[2] Tiffany argued, "That is exactly why she was killed—because of gender identity."[3] In a videotaped interview submitted to the court, Tiffany stated, "If a person gets mad at you for being transgender and then comes back and kills you because his pride was crushed, and he was interested in someone he thought was a woman, it's a hate crime."[4] The suspect, Henry R. Gleaves, a 20-year-old black cisgender man who Edwards met online ambushed her in a hotel hallway after learning that she was a transgender woman. Gleaves claimed during his trial that he paid Edwards for sex believing he was soliciting services from a biologically born female. Tiffany told *Buzzfeed* in a phone interview, "Tell them you're a tranny; they will get mad and retaliate in front of a group because they didn't (sic) want people to think differently of them."[5]

Gleaves concocted a self-defense story as his defense claiming that Edwards and three others attacked and robbed him. The jury found Gleaves guilty of second-degree manslaughter and tampering with evidence, and he was sentenced to seven years in prison.[6] While a form of justice was served, the jury did not return a murder conviction. In the closing arguments, the prosecuting attorney, John Balenovich, who used Papi's birth name throughout the entire trial, misgendering her in death, said, "[Gleaves] chose to kill Sherman Edwards because he was humiliated, and he got his money taken."[7]

In a comparable situation, 30-year-old Lamia Beard was murdered from multiple gunshot wounds. Responding to a 911 call at 4 a.m., her body was found on a sidewalk and transported to a nearby hospital where she later died. Media outlets reported that transgender sex workers were known to work in the area. Most of these outlets identified Beard as a man. Unfortunately, no suspect to date has been identified for the crime. According to Osman Ahmed, National Coalition of Anti-Violence Programs (NCAVP)'s Research and Education Coordinator at the New York City Anti-Violence Project, in discussing her death:

> Lamia's death is a tremendous loss, and tragedy so early in the year is a painful reminder of the disproportionate violence that transgender women of color face.
>
> We need immediate action on a national level to address this epidemic of violence against transgender women, so that in the days, and weeks and months ahead we are not issuing these alerts because our community members are no longer being killed."[8]

The murders of Tyra Underwood and Yazmin Vash Payne are eerily similar. Both were victims of intimate partner violence (IPV) by black cisgender men. On the morning of January 26, a 21-year-old black cisgender man, Carlton Ray Champion Jr., gunned down 24-year-old Underwood in her car. Champion Jr. was a football player at Texas College, a historically black college in Tyler, Texas. The two met on the popular internet chat service, Kik, and had been dating for several weeks. During this period, Champion Jr. and Underwood had become sexually involved. According to the arrest warrant affidavit, the day before Champion Jr. murdered Underwood he had become upset because Underwood no longer wanted to date him. Underwood wrote in her Kik message:

> Carlton bro you saw me kiking you at 11:00 [p.m.] but you chose to be with whoever you was with and no (sic) you think you can just fuck with me when you want.[9]

After a series of messages, the two agreed to meet on a random street after midnight. Police officers responded to the scene at approximately 2:26 a.m. to discover that Underwood had been shot several times while inside of her car. The arrest warrant affidavit indicated that Champion Jr. intentionally and knowingly murdered her.[10] During the trial, his attorney presented a trans panic defense claiming he was unaware that Underwood was a transgender woman. Even Underwood's mother did not help the prosecution's case. When testifying she used male pronouns by stating on the stand, "He was a pretty good kid, smart kid. He was always honest. He was a normal little boy, he liked stuff little boys liked."[11]

After being convicted of life in prison, Champion Jr. yelled out in the courtroom, "I'm going to be back on the streets" showing little remorse for the death of Underwood.[12] Speaking to the local media after the trial, Underwood's roommate, Coy Simmons, argued, "This has to be a hate crime, this has to be a hate crime, nothing else because that was an upstanding person with a good heart."[13] Despite Simmons's claim, this was not considered a hate-based crime.

In similar circumstances, 33-year-old Yazmin Vash Payne was stabbed to death by her 25-year-old black cisgender boyfriend, Ezekiel J. Dear. Escorted by his pastor, Dear turned himself into law enforcement officials the following day and confessed to the murder of Payne. The two had recently moved into a one-bedroom apartment together. After murdering her, Dear set their apartment on fire. Her body was found around 5 a.m. No solid motive was ever established in the case, yet neighbors reported hearing the two arguing late into the night. During the trial, Dear pled not guilty although confessing to the murder. In December of 2016, he was sentenced to 13 years in prison convicted of voluntary manslaughter and arson.

In the four tragic scenarios described above, black transgender women were senselessly murdered. Did their gender identities lead them to be victims of hate-based violence, intimate partner violence, and sex work related violence? By virtue of the available details, we make inference that their gender identities played an important role in their deaths. But, how do we address these forms of structural and cultural violence? Based on national reports and past literature, the most troubling problem to these questions is that these women, and numerous others, have yet to receive any dignified form of justice. Thus, in this chapter, I ask: *How, who, why, and do? How* do we explain the transphobic violence and murders of black transgender women? *Who* is committing these violence acts? Beyond the question of *who* is *why* do these murders continue? *Do* the collective societal and cultural identities that embody their very existence continue to harm their ability to live in safe spaces?

According to Collins (1990; 2000), in her work that examines the multiple dimensions of black womanhood, such gender-based violence must be understood using an intersectional approach that examines the power relations of each socially and culturally constructed identity rather than as a set of independent experiences. The better we understand these relationships, the more likely we can find appropriate solutions to this epidemic. As we have seen, there is a deliberate practice of intersectional erasure within the black community and in the larger American society, which leads to the most substantive question: *Do black transgender women lives matter?*

Similar to gender-based violence against black cisgender women, black transgender women are also vulnerable to the same violent acts of gender violence. The divergence between the two groups is that black transgender women are most victimized for their refusal to adhere to societal, cultural, and gender norms. According to Witten and Eyler (1997, p. 3) in their presentation of transgender-related hate crimes:

> Perpetrators often believe that a person who transgresses the norms of gendered sexuality, either by engaging in sexual relationships with members of the *"non-opposite"* gender, or by behaving *"as"* the other gender, is deviant or morally defective, and thus a deserving victim of violence and aggression.

Such patriarchal violence fueled by heteronormative attitudes and beliefs leads to the "they deserved it" theory as Witten and Eyler (1999, p. 461) found in their research on hate-based crimes and violence against transgender people. When situating this epidemic within the black community, black cisgender men, who are said to commit an absorbent amount of transphobic violence and murders, operate as if their acts against black transgender women are merely an act of justifiable masculinity. The effects of patriarchy lead these cisgender men to perform violent acts through hate-based violence, intimate partner violence, and violence against transgender sex workers. The purpose of this chapter is to apply an intersectional approach to explore the situational and cultural contexts that lead to the transphobic violence and murders of these women.

The Intersectionality of Black Trans Women

To properly address the continued transphobic violence and murders of black transgender women, an intersectional approach through the prism of black feminist theory provides sensibility to this wide-ranging problem. The framework of intersectionality is rooted in black feminist theory. From Beale (1970) and Bond and Perry (1970) who introduced the framework of "double jeopardy" to describe the dual discrimination of racism and sexism to King (1988, p. 47) who expanded the framework to "multiple jeopardy" which included classism to explain "simultaneous oppressions" as well as "the multiplicative relationships among them" that lead to the exploitation of black women, the paradigm of intersectionality related to black women began with a solid foundation.

Davis (2008, p. 68) defines intersectionality as "the interaction between gender, race, and other categories of difference in individual lives, social practices, institutional arrangements, and cultural ideologies and the outcomes of these interactions in terms of power." Davis's definition builds on Crenshaw (1989), who in her groundbreaking essay served to demarginalize the intersection of race and sex, coined the term "intersectionality." In the essay, she explains that past studies which used a "single-axis framework erase Black women" because they fail to take into account the multiple forms of oppression faced by these women (p. 140). By expanding, she suggests that it would create an appropriate framework that accounts for the combined race-based and gender-based forms of discrimination interlocked at the center of their experiences.[14] Crenshaw explains in an interview for the book, *The Intersectional Approach*:

> [M]y own use of the term 'intersectionality' was just a metaphor. [...] I was simply looking at the way all of these systems of oppression overlap. But more importantly, how in the process of that structural convergence rhetorical politics and identity politics—based on the idea that systems of subordination do not overlap—would abandon issues and causes and people who actually were affected by overlapping systems of subordination. (Berger and Guidroz 2010, p. 65)

In a 1991 essay titled, *Mapping the Margins*, Crenshaw introduces three forms of intersectionality to explore "the race and gender dimensions of violence against women of color" (p. 1242). She set out to study how race and gender dimensions intersect with the facets of structural, political, and representational intersectionalities to explain aspects of violence. The first is "structural intersectionality." This concept refers to "the ways in which the location of women of color at the intersection of race and gender makes our actual experience of domestic violence, rape, and remedial reform qualitatively different than that of white women" (p. 1245). The second is "political intersectionality." This concept suggests, "both feminist and antiracist politics" have worked together "to marginalize the issue of violence against women of color" (p. 1245). The last is "representational intersectionality." This concept looks at "the cultural construction of women of color" drawing on racist and sexist representations that marginalize women of color (p. 1245 and p. 1283). Crenshaw concludes, that while the framing of the various interactions of race and gender in the context of violence is useful in our understanding, intersectionality might be more "useful as a way of mediating the tension between assertions of multiple identity and the ongoing necessity of group politics" (p. 1296).

The work of Crenshaw and others allow us to reconceptualize the patriarchal and heteronormative frames that conflate race, gender, socioeconomic status, and other identities related to women of color. As mentioned, Collins (1990; 2000), in her work that examines the multiple dimensions of black womanhood, believes that such gender-based violence must be understood using an intersectional approach. In a later study attempting to develop a black feminist praxis, Collins (2003) offers the concept of intersectionality as a heuristic to understand the context of group dynamics. The heuristic approach allows intersectionality "the ability of social phenomena such as race, class, and gender to mutually construct one another" (p. 205). She introduces the standpoint theory that proposes that group location in hierarchical power structures produces shared challenges for individuals in those groups (p. 201). For example, race and gender create a fixed identity which situates black women in the lower tier of the hierarchy of the group, thus, as stated in Chapter 1, must be addressed to continue a generative power of black solidarity that views all black people as equal.

A plethora of research has emerged on intersectionality across disciplines since Crenshaw addressing the concerns of black women. While intersectionality offers an analytic viewpoint to examine the dimensions of marginalization faced by women of color and black women, scholars have argued that the tenets of intersectionality at times constitute an incomplete framework (see Davis 2008; Rahman 2010; Anthias 2013; Patil 2013). These works maintain that intersectionality must not be reduced into a single social division, but rather, expanded to deal with the complexity of power constructions.

bell hooks (2000, 2004) in her discussion of intersectional constructs suggest that intersectionality as an approach often falls short of the goal because patriarchy continues to loom which ultimately carries on systems of oppression. In her development of the term "imperialist white supremacist capitalist patriarchy," hooks argues that patriarchy is the connector that interlocks political systems. Patriarchy functions as a political-social system that allows the constructs of racism, sexism, and classism to act as oppressive mechanisms (2004, p. 18). hooks explains how these constructs, which are interrelated constructs of our social structure within the context of power, function as systems of oppression and inevitably affect access to societal and cultural acceptance.

From the approaches of Crenshaw and hooks, it is the work of Collins (2004) who attempts to distinguish between the perspectives of "intersectional" and "interlocking," which allows us to view the issues and concerns of black women from a macro-level and micro-level. Collins et al. (1995) explains in their article, *Doing Difference*:

> [T]he notion of interlocking oppressions refers to macro level connections linking systems of oppression such as race, class, and gender. This is the model describing the social structures that create social positions. Second, the notion of intersectionality describes micro-level processes—namely, how each individual and group occupies a social position within interlocking structures of oppression described by the metaphor of intersectionality. Together they shape oppression. (p. 492)

In a later analysis, Collins (2000, p. 299) argues that intersectionality is the "analysis claiming that systems of race, social class, gender, sexuality, ethnicity, nation, and age form mutually constructing features of social organization, which shape Black women's experiences and, in turn, are shaped by Black women." Her assessment of macro-level and micro-level processes allows for a more holistic study of the lived experiences of black women, and germane to this book, grants the latitude to as well study black transgender women.

I believe, an approach that is interlocking and intersectional, can offer valuable insight to frame the situational and contextual experiences of black transgender women. In a unique way, this approach brings together the intersections of race, gender identity, and socioeconomic status, while understanding

that a looming interlocking system of power that is preceded by the authoritative nature of patriarchy affects their day-to-day lives. This collaborative
platform engages the complex identities of black transgender women as human
beings within the black community and in the larger American society and
allows us to develop and build upon methods to address the multidimensional
nature of oppression.

de Vries (2012), in his article on intersectional identities of transgender people, argues that when transgender people transition, despite being
in a dominant white culture or ethnic culture, there is social and cultural
resistance to their new identity. In a later intersectional study that examined
transgender people of color experiences in the USA, de Vries (2014) found
that barriers against transgender people are predicated on their interconnect-
ing social positions. All five of the black transgender women in the study
"experienced further marginalization for occupying a transgender status in
connection with their racial identity" (p. 20). He concluded that transgender
people of color are hindered by "some of the ways race, ethnicity, social class,
gender, sexuality, body size, nationality, and language interconnect and are
attributed institutionalized meanings by others" (p. 20).

In spite of the gender and gender identity perceptive differences between
black cisgender women and black transgender women, the macro-level and
micro-level intersectional approach is most applicable to explain the forms of
gender-based violence deep-seated in the structures of patriarchy that often
disregards the humanity of both women.[15] When used as a praxis applied to
black transgender women, such an approach allows the ability to understand
better how the collective constructs "intersect at the micro level of individual
experience to reflect multiple interlocking systems of privilege and oppression at the macro social-structural level" (Bowleg 2012, p. 1267). When the
micro and macro levels intersect, it produces negative societal and cultural
outcomes for black transgender women.

According to Sarah McBride, who is a transgender woman and the
National Press Secretary for the Human Rights Campaign (HRC), "When
homophobia, racism, sexism, and transphobia are combined, it can have fatal
or deadly consequences. Because of all of the different prejudices that trans
women of color can face with their intersecting identities, it has often put
them at the crosshairs of hate."[16] McBride's stance echoes that of Laverne
Cox, who argued in a 2014 interview with *Democracy Now!* that, "It's important to look at the intersectional piece, that we're usually talking about trans
women of color, that there's something about—that black bodies are under
attack in this culture, and black trans bodies are under attack."[17]

There are distinctive life experiences that black transgender women go through within the black community and in the larger American society. Everything considered, the intersectionality between their race, gender identity, and socioeconomic status poses the most significant threat to gendered forms of acceptance.[18] On the micro-level, their identity is challenged when these multiple intersections function simultaneously, and a host of "isms" and "phobias" are calculated by alleged heterosexual demigods to disprove of their being. On the macro-level, the interlocking systems of oppression attempt to maintain a societal, cultural, and gender norm of masculinity negating transgender acceptance.

While it is known that the summation of the multiple intersections of their life experiences are used against them to appropriate their placement in a gender-socialized American society and black patriarchal culture, this book continues to argue that black transgender women should be viewed as *women* worthy of a living, breathing status, and not marginalized by these collective intersections. Thus, an intersectional perspective is needed to increase our understanding of the societal and cultural exclusions that operate within certain contexts to continue the violence against these women.

Hate-Based Violence

The Civil Rights Act of 1968, also known as the Fair Housing Act, was the first piece of federal legislation signed into law to help protect citizens from hate-based violence.[19] Such hate crime legislation evolved over time at the federal and state levels of government initially protecting citizens on the basis of race, ethnicity, gender, disability, and religion. On April 23, 1990, the U.S. Congress passed the Hate Crime Statistics Act due to the growing concern of hate-based violence. Under this Act, hate crimes were defined as an offense "that manifest evidence of prejudice based on race, religion, sexual orientation, or ethnicity."[20]

In 2005, black U.S. Representative John Conyers, Jr. (D-MI) introduced the Local Law Enforcement Hate Crimes Prevention Act. Under this Act, hate crimes would have expanded to cover gender, sexual orientation, gender identity, and disability. Legislators on both sides of the political aisle introduced multiple versions of this legislation over the years. Finally, in 2009 both the U.S. House and U.S. Senate, along with provisions from the Department of Defense (DOD), passed the bill in both chambers. On October 28, 2009, former President Barack H. Obama signed, "The Matthew Shepard and James Byrd, Jr., Hate Crimes Prevention Act," which widened the categories of victims to include "perceived gender, disability, sexual orientation, or gender identity of any person."[21]

After the passage of this Act, Republican Vice-President and former Indiana governor, Mike Pence, lobbied against its intent when he was a U.S. congressional member. He stated:

> The issue of hate crimes legislation that continues to be advanced on Capitol Hill is part of a larger effort that we already see working in state statutes. And however well intentioned, hate crimes statutes around the country have been used to quell religious expression. Individual pastors who may wish to preach out of Romans Chapter 1 about what the Bible teaches about homosexual behavior ... could be charged or subject to intimidation for simply expressing a biblical moral view on the issue of homosexual behavior.[22]

Pence's conservative stance was devoid of credible information regarding the functionality of hate-based crimes, but rather, his intent was to control the influence of LGBTQIA activists. His statement did not positively acknowledge the inclusion of language for sexual orientation and gender identity and expression into the new federal hate crimes law.

Under this Act, local law enforcement officials would be given training and resources from the federal government to identify better and report hate-based violence. Moreover, these officials were now responsible for gathering hate crime statistics motivated by gender identity to gain a useful understanding of where, why, and how do such violence and murders continue to affect transgender and gender non-conformity people. But reporting hate-based crimes to the federal government has not come without much criticism.

In 2014, for the first time, the FBI released its annual Hate Crime Statistics report of hate crimes based on gender identity (i.e., transgender and gender non-conformity).[23] The report found that of the 5,922 single-bias incidents reported in 2013, the top three bias categories were race (48.5%), sexual orientation (20.8%), and religion (17.4%). Gender identity (0.5%) and gender (0.3%) ranked last. Only 31 people[24] were reportedly victimized based on gender identity and 18 based on gender.[25] In stark contrast, the NCAVP released a similar report based on 2012 data finding that 344 transgender people had been victimized.[26] In their report, more than two-thirds of murder victims were transgender women. Sixty-seven percent of these victims were transgender women of color.[27] The disparity led to a national outcry from transgender activists. According to Raffi Freedman-Gurspan, a policy adviser for the National Center on Transgender Equity (NCTE), "We've had people's genitals mutilated after they're dead. It's absolutely rooted in transphobia and hatred and it's absolutely a national crisis."[28]

The following year, the FBI report showed an increase from 31 reported in 2013 to 114 in 2015.[29] Transgender activists contend that transgender and gender non-conformity people may be the most victimized by hate-based violence in the USA and these statistics are grossly underreported due to a patriarchal mentality among law enforcement officers and agencies when reporting such crimes. A significant number of law enforcement agencies in the USA did not report any data based on gender identity. Prior to the Hate Crimes Prevention Act, Stotzer (2009), in her study of violence against transgender people in the USA, found that while 45 states and the District of Columbia had hate crime laws on the books, none of the ten states included in her research that had "gender identity bias" as a recognized category ever reported such crimes.[30]

In a 2016 report from the Associated Press that analyzed hate crime data from 2009 to 2014, they found "more than 2,700 city police and county sheriff's departments across the country that [had] not submitted a single hate crime report for the FBI's annual crime tally during the past six years."[31] The gross underreporting by the FBI and other law enforcement agencies is an egregious act systematically embedded in a patriarchal structured criminal justice system. This is especially disconcerting following the 2016 Pulse nightclub shooting and the upheaval of hate-based crimes after the election of President Donald J. Trump.

On June 12, 2016, a gunman opened fire at the Pulse nightclub in Orlando, Florida claiming the lives of 49 people and injuring 53 other people. LGBTQIA activists and people were devastated following the massacre at the gay nightclub, which was a hate-based attack aimed directly at the LGBTQIA community. This mass shooting is considered one of the deadliest in modern-day U.S. history. Human Rights Campaign (HRC) president, Chad Griffin, said in response to this hate-based crime:

> We are devastated by this tragic act of violence, which has reportedly claimed the lives of at least 50 LGBTQ people and allies and injured more than 50 others. We are grieving for the victims and our hearts are broken for their friends, families, and for the entire community. This tragedy has occurred as our community celebrates pride, and now more than ever we must come together as a nation to affirm that love conquers hate.[32]

After the November 8, 2016, election of President Donald J. Trump, the number of hate-based crimes rose exponentially.[33] In the ten days following his election to office, the Southern Poverty Law Center (SPLC) estimated 876 new cases in the USA.[34] LGBTQIA activists argued that President Trump's explicit anti-LGBTQIA rhetoric during the campaign trail correlated to the 95 (11%) LGBTQIA-related hate crimes incidents.[35]

The transgender community's vulnerability is tied to these statistics.[36] Without the appropriate statistics, it is difficult to combat transphobic attitudes and beliefs that propel such crimes. Perry (2003), in her research on hate-based crimes, argues that, "without the raw materials, there is no foundation for theorizing" (p. 14). Despite the most recent 2015 USTS not categorizing hate-based crimes, the survey did report that 48% of transgender people responded that they had been denied equal treatment, were verbally harassed, and/or physically attacked, all categories known to comprise hate-based crimes, in the past year due to their gender identity.[37]

Even with the increased attention to hate-based violence against transgender and gender non-conforming people, the black transgender women interviewed argued that the enactment of legislation will not deter those who desire to commit such crimes.[38] They insisted that heterosexual and cisgender men exercise these bias motivated crimes as a mechanism of power and oppression to maintain a rigid gender order.[39] The women were unmoved in their belief that hate-based legislation could slow this epidemic due to its multi-dimensions varying from verbal abuse, physical violence, sexual violence, murder to overkill. In their opinion, there is no safe-haven for transgender people. They believed that the best options are for them to become hypervigilant to their surroundings and practice behaviors and routines to protect themselves. According to Alexandria Sweet:

> You have the real police and then you have the gender police. I don't know which one is worse. A black cis man once kicked my ass for just speaking to him. I said, 'hello.' Then all I know is that I was on the ground getting pounded. He beat the shit out of me. I was in the hospital for a week. Months later I saw the man. I went and told a police officer. The officer was like, 'Oh well, did you tell him you were a man?'

The description of the hate-based violence against Alexandria points to the rigid gender binary that protects hegemonic masculinity and uses physical violence to maintain heterosexuality as the societal, cultural, and gender norms (see Perry 2001; Kelley and Gruenewald 2014; Lee and Kwan 2014; Smyth and Jenness 2014). Barbara Perry (2001), who is often referred to as the pioneer for the inclusion of intersectionality to explain accounts of hate-based crimes, argues that such crimes allow a way for men to exert their masculinity. Kelley and Gruenewald (2014), in their study of the fatal attacks against LGBTQ people across different situational circumstances, found that in most cases male offenders use violence to demonstrate hegemonic masculinity. As their study applied hegemonic masculinity to such fatal acts, they argue it is possible that in certain situational contexts "men of different racial and ethnic backgrounds draw from different social structures informing them how to "be a man," which affects their use or disuse of violence" (p. 23).

This rigid gender binary has also shown to defend the male offender in hate-based crimes after their victimization of transgender women. For instance, the institutional practice of "blaming the victim" because "she tricked me" allows the male offender to defend his masculinity. Lee and Kwan (2014), in their study of trans panic defense (or also known as the "You tricked me" defense), explain that offenders often present this defense in a court of law. Male offenders argue that a bias motivated murder toward a transgender woman resulted from discovering her (or his) gender identity in the aftermath of a physical or sexual encounter. These offenders often claim "temporary insanity, provocation, or self-defense" on the basis that a transgender woman is not a "real" woman (p. 80).[40] Their defense relies on victim blaming which labels the victim as a "deceiver" rather than a "victim" (Buist and Stone 2014). Lee and Kwan (2014) concluded that the trans panic defense is tied to hegemonic masculinity in that, "killing the transgender woman reinforces and affirms the defendant's masculine identity" (p. 110).

In certain cases, hate-based violence against transgender people is characterized by what law enforcement officials refer to as "overkill". This term is "defined as injuries inflicted on a victim, more than what is necessary to cause that victims death" (Drake 2004, p. 332). Transgender activist, Gwendolyn Ann Smith, also the founder of the Transgender Day of Remembrance (TDoR), in her now-defunct online blog, "Remembering Our Died Project" specified that overkill, "Gets to a point where it's not just about killing a person. It is about obliterating them, erasing them if you could."[41]

Naomi Mars, in her reflection of the hate-based violence she has endured since transitioning, provided a horrifying description of one experience early in her transition:

> The worse case of random violence that has happened to me came about two years after I transitioned. I didn't quite know the rules of the game. For example, places that I could or couldn't go. How to become invisible in the presence of black cis men. I definitely didn't know how to sense danger.

To make a long story short, I was in Family Dollar getting a couple of things. There were two guys there shopping who kept whispering and looking at me. I could hear one of the guys say, 'That's a dude.' When I heard that, I should have left immediately or at least made sure that I left before them. When I was walking to my car that was kinda on the side of the building, one of them approached me and asked, 'Do you have a dick?' He maybe asked me two to three times. But I kept ignoring him and was trying to hurry to get into my car. Then, bam! He cold-cocked me. When I was on the ground, he spit on me and kicked the shit out of me repeatedly. This side of my face was swollen the size of a grapefruit. He said so many hateful things to me while I was on the ground. Then he started to pull out his dick and piss on me but his homeboy was like come on.

Naomi's story is similar to many of the women interviewed who explained that they were the victims of random hate-based violence on several occasions. According to Bobbie Golden, "It would be difficult to find one black trans woman in the world who hasn't gotten her ass beat or come very close to getting her ass beat for no reason except that she is trans. These streets are not safe for us." She goes on to expound that:

Let me tell you about one situation. I came outside to find that someone had spray-painted 'tranny' on my car. My car was white too and the paint was red. I believe that a trick followed me back to my apartment and did it. We had exchanged words because he tried to short me on my money. He was a first-timer and a little unsure of how it all went.

I was so embarrassed [when I saw my car spray-painted]. I had just moved to that neighborhood so, few people knew me. Much less that I was trans. Later that night when I got home, there was a [black] guy sitting on the stairs leading to my apartment. When I tried to walk past him, he grabbed me and said, 'I know what you are.' He forced his way into my apartment and brutally raped me. He choked me until I almost fainted. I had bruises and scratches on my back from him literally pounding my back with his fists and scratching and digging into my skin while raping me from the back. I suffered severe anal fissure.

That was the first time that I wanted to commit suicide. I remember wanting to call my mother but like I told you she had disowned me.

All the black transgender women interviewed agreed that the hate that motivates human-on-human violence will continue to intensify as we are witness to the coming out and/or transition of more and more black transgender women. Similar to Meyer (2010, p. 991), in his study of evaluating the severity of LGBTQ hate-based experiences, the women felt that physical violence based on their gender identity motivated by hate, regardless of the situational and cultural contexts, has "caused them more pain than any of their other violent experiences." Meyer does point out that rather than placing violence in hierarchical terms, we should deem all forms of violence as equally harmful. Bobbie Golden made clear in her response that:

> I've been beaten in relationships and in hotel rooms by crazy motherfuckers [who committed violence against me]. But when you are choked, beaten, and raped just because you chose to identify as a woman it hurts because I can't control that. This is who I am. This man forced his way into my apartment and had his way with me. He wasn't my boyfriend. He didn't pay me for my services. He targeted me because I'm a trans woman.

> Look at that trans woman [Zella Ziona] who has lured into the ally and shot in the head and private area. That was nothing but hate.

In October of 2015, 21-year-old, Zella Ziona, was the 16th black transgender woman murdered. Her body was found in a service alley behind a shopping center. Twenty-year-old, Rico H. LeBlond reportedly murdered Ziona because she subjected him to embarrassment by flirting with him in front of his male friends. In a police statement, "Witnesses said that after initially shooting [Ziona], the suspect walked over to her, stood over her, and fired more rounds into her body."[42] LeBlond was charged with first-degree murder despite family and friends advocating for a hate-crime charge. It was later learned that the two had been acquaintances since middle school. During the interview with Bobbie Golden, the details of the case had just been released. Disappointingly, on January 13, 2017, a jury failed to reach a unanimous verdict in the case. They deadlocked 10–2 in favor of a first-degree conviction. Afterwards, the judge, Anne Albright, declared a mistrial.

HRC president, Chad Griffin, said of the hate-based crimes against transgender women in 2015:

> Transgender people, especially transgender women of color, continue to be targeted in vicious attacks all throughout this country. The simple act of walking down the street is cause for real fear and anti-transgender political rhetoric only serves to embolden those who harass and intimidate people simply because of who they are.[43]

Ending hate-based violence against black transgender women will be an arduous task. Therefore, the push to lower the amount of hate-based violence directed toward them must be met head-on with legislation and advocacy to discourage the rate of "gender policing" in the USA.

Intimate Partner Violence (IPV)

In the context of intimate partner violence (IPV), Alexandria Sweet explained that, "In a relationship, we get the same domestic abuse that cis women get. There's no difference. Violence against women is violence against women no matter if you're trans or not. In my opinion, we just get more of it." In the discussion of IPV among the black transgender women, all of them indicated that the endeavor of dating a cisgender or heterosexual man has been problematic. Jae Palmer, who detransitioned, provided a comparison:

> Lets be real, we all know that violence against women symbolizes male power to them. This is really true when it comes to trans women.

> We say partner violence but we should really say genitalia violence. If a trans woman is passable, then the only people who really know day in and day out [that she is trans], are the people in the relationship. The violence comes from the fact that the two of you have the same body part. One person feels like they have to control the other.

The Centers for Disease Control and Prevention (CDC) define the term "intimate partner violence" as "physical violence, sexual violence, stalking and psychological aggression (including coercive acts) by a current or former intimate partner."[44] In a 2013 comprehensive report titled, *Intimate Partner Violence: Attributes Of Victimization, 1993–2011*, the Bureau of Justice Statistics (BJS), defines it as "rape or sexual assault, robbery, aggravated assault, and simple assault committed by the victim's current or former spouse, boyfriend, or girlfriend."[45] These definitions provide an operational context to better understand how IPV is defined and its application to the comparability of gender-based violence between cisgender women and transgender women.

In the 2015 USTS, 54% of transgender people had experienced some form of IPV.[46] This survey follows another 2015 study of IPV and sexual abuse among LGBTQIA people, in which the *Williams Institute* found that transgender people are victimized at a higher rate than the total gender population.[47] In their compilation of 42 past research studies, from 1989 to 2015, they established that LGBTQIA people experience a lifetime of IPV. For transgender people, between 31 and 50% experience IPV in their lifetime.[48]

The prevalence of IPV toward black transgender women is made worse by the intersections of race, gender identity, and socioeconomic status. The sum total of these negative factors triggers a daily assault on the lives of black transgender women and harmfully affects the perception of their cultural identity. Edwards et al. (2015), in their overview and critical analysis of research on IPV, found increased rates of IPV among sexual minorities. According to Venus Love, who discussed these intersections along with the mental health outcome of IPV, explained:

> If I hear, 'you're a man, but you look so much like a woman' one more damn time. That's a precursor to the violence. It's hard for a black cis man to date me because psychologically he won't ever be able to get over the fact that I was biologically born male, and sexually it will be hard for him because he will always be measuring his penis length versus mine to measure his own masculinity. Not literally but figuratively. Well, maybe literally.

> If he's a *Top*, Lord don't let me get a hard-on during sex. It will scare him to death. Not because I'm turned on but because he'll think I want to use it on him. If they're a *Top* only, it may lead to a violent altercation in the bedroom and outside of the bedroom.

> The rest of the day he'll say demeaning things to me to make himself feel better. In one relationship, I accepted that abuse for a long time because I confused tolerance with love. I was depressed after we broke up because I allowed him to tear me completely down.

In a black patriarchal culture, the IPV experienced by black cisgender women often identically mirrors the violence experienced by black transgender women. Venus goes on to expound on her story:

> What I just told you was really no different than a cis woman's story. What's crazy about that story is that [the black cisgender man who I was in a relationship with] ex-girlfriend popped up at my place one day and we had a real good discussion. He beat her just like he beat me. Their problems also started in the bedroom. He used violence to control her and me.

Such violence against black transgender women brings to our attention the continual need to address the lack of meaningful accountability of gendered violence within the black community. Moreover, it establishes a need to present a transcultural context to the application of the definition to dissect the distinctive types of IPV that these women experience (Ruiz-Perez et al. 2007).

Sexual violence within the relationship represents only one dimension of the types of victimization these women experience. Testa et al. (2012), in their study of the effects of violence on transgender people, found that while 27% of the respondents reported sexual violence, 38% reported surviving physical violence. The transgender women who survived physical violence were five times more likely to report a suicide attempt. As revealed in the preceding chapters, survivors of such domestic abuse have higher than average rates of suicidal thoughts and attempted suicide.

The black transgender women interviewed indicated that there were, at times, an inexplicable "aggressive awakening" from some of the men who they dated in the past to exercise masculine control. According to Sophie Rush:

> I once had a [black] boyfriend beat my ass because I spoke to his son. His baby momma had dropped the boy off to the apartment. He wanted me to stay in the room so the little boy wouldn't see me. I said, 'Cool.' Well, the little boy ran into the bedroom right after I had gotten out of the shower. In a panic, I said, 'Hi' and he ran out. Later that night, I got a good ole fashion ass beatin'. He told me he didn't want his son to know that I existed.

Arianna Gray in her scenario of an "aggressive awakening" described a brief relationship with a [white] pansexual man from college that ended with her on the receiving end of a black eye. She described that they had dated for about a month before his violent tendencies toward her began to show. Struggling to disclose this information through tears, she stated:

> It's really plain and simple. He wanted to control me. After a month of dating, he started to verbally intimidate me by telling me I wasn't a 'real woman' and calling me a 'tranny'. During sex he would pull off my wig and call me by my government name. When I told him the relationship wouldn't work for me anymore, he punched me in my eye.

> What is most bizarre about the story is that even when we broke up, he did things to torment me. When I started dating another guy [who was black], he wrote a humiliating letter about me and placed it on my new boyfriend's windshield. That was really childish. He [my new boyfriend] cursed me out and hemmed me up but he didn't hit me.

> About a year later, a friend contacted me and said he saw pictures of me on the Plenty of Fish site [dating website]. They were pictures we [pansexual boyfriend] took together but, he cropped himself out. He was a major asshole.

The normalization of IPV in transgender relationships is a grave concern. Sevelius (2013), in her study of risk behaviors of transgender women of color, makes the case that "gender affirmation" among transgender women is needed for support of their gender identity. However, a high need for gender affirmation combined with low access to outlets for positive gender affirmation leads to these volatile relationships. Arianna Gray in her concluding assessment of IPV pointed out, "This violence happened to me from a guy I met at school.

Can you imagine if I had met him on the street? The need to be loved is real for trans women."

Black transgender women's vulnerability to IPV and the decision to remain in the relationship is a multi-faceted discussion. One that ranges from low social status, social entrapment, battered women's syndrome, isolation from family and friends, outing, to mere acceptance of their gender identity (see Greenberg 2012). The "Why didn't you leave?" rationale of thinking is difficult to apply to a group of human beings who desire gender affirmation, when it is believed, that they have found someone to not only accept them but love them.

Take, for example, the Yazmin Vash Payne case. The night of her murder was not the first domestic dispute between Payne and her boyfriend, Ezekiel J. Dear. Witnesses had heard them arguing on other occasions, but they were silent. That night a physical altercation with her boyfriend left Payne on the kitchen floor with multiple stab wounds to the torso. To hide his toxic act, he set the apartment on fire. Following his crimes of IPV and alleged hate, in the most daunting act, he entered the police department the following day with his pastor, who is the archetypal symbol of patriarchy and religious messenger of heteronormative actions and behaviors, to turn himself in to authorities.

Violence and Murders against Transgender Sex Workers

The sex trade profession is considered the world's oldest profession. This American past time offers a conduit to make an earning for those ostracized from the traditional workplace due to non-employment, mistreatment and discrimination, denial of promotion, or firing. For black transgender women who are forced into this profession due to economic necessity, many are labeled with a stigma that is used to characterize their actions as criminal and immoral as opposed to addressing the systemic, institutional, and inter-personal circumstances that make this employment option a labor issue. This faulty lens paints the sex trade profession as a monolithic occupation for all transgender women. This book contends that transgender sex workers, and transgender women in general, are valuable members of our society and must not be labeled for their participation in the sex trade profession.

In the 2011 NTDS, the transgender unemployment rate was estimated to be 14%.[49] When controlling for race, the unemployment rate was 28% for black transgender people.[50] As a result, 53% of black transgender people had extremely high rates of participating in sex work for income.[51] As mentioned

in Chapter 1, in the 2015 joint report led by the NCTE, 44% of black transgender women and 33% of Latina transgender women were more likely to
engage in sex work than their white counterparts.[52]

In the 2015 USTS, high rates of unemployment also led transgender
women to be more likely to participate in the sex trade profession as street-
based sex workers and escorts. The survey found that black transgender women
(42%), American Indian transgender women (28%), multiracial transgender
women (27%), Latina transgender women (23%), and Asian transgender
women (22%) were more likely to have participated in sex work for income.
The USTS reported that in the previous year, black transgender women were
five times more likely to have performed sex work for income and 48% worked
exclusively on the street.[53] These alarming figures speak to the reason why a
significant number of transgender women of all racial and ethnic makeups,
who may have toiled at other jobs in the past and been subjected to discriminatory practices, are eventually forced to enter a life of transgender sex work.

Venus Love, who described that sex work is not a beloved choice for most
black transgender women, also argued that these women should be able to
work in safe environments. She articulated:

> After high school, I took a job working at the mall. I was on the verge of transition-
> ing. When I finally decided to transition fully, I was fired the next day. The manager
> asked me to come in the back room for a talk. When we got there, he told me that
> my dress was against company policy. I looked for a job for over a year. No one would
> hire me. I tried college but I got harassed everyday. Eventually, I said, 'fuck it' and
> tried the lifestyle.
>
> Ever since, it's been hell. I've been raped, beaten, and arrested. You name it, it's
> happened to me. The messed up thing about it is that police officers harass us just
> as much as the cis men soliciting us. I once told a police officer I was raped, and he
> forced himself on me while I was trying to get his help.

In her response, Venus also pinpointed the systemic and institutional railroad-
ing of black transgender women from the workplace to street-based sex workers
and escorts. She further explained that, "Presenting myself as a woman has
been hard on my life. I think I'm a fairly intelligent person. I could hold down
a [traditional] job. But when I put on this wig, people only see trans, freak, etc."

The black transgender women interviewed agreed that the sex trade profession is highly stigmatized. They believed that deleterious labels attached to
their decision to participate in this profession should be reserved due to the
negative circumstances that lead to them choosing it "as a means of economic

survival." According to Naomi Mars when explaining this mislabeling, "What would society have liked for me to do? My family disowned me. I was homeless. I couldn't get a job. Don't demonize me. Help me. Instead, you cut my leg off and ask me to walk within society without being noticed."[54] Operario et al. (2008), in their meta-analysis on sex work and HIV status among transgender women that aggregated the results of 25 past studies, concurred with Naomi's position that during life turning points, transgender women need help. In their research, the authors concluded that structural and social network-based interventions would help to reduce their dependence on the sex trade profession as a method of economic survival and reduce sexual assaults. The 2015 USTS reported that 72% of transgender women who have done sex work had been sexually assaulted in their lifetimes.[55]

As the national reports and past literature have shown, transgender women of color, especially black transgender women, who enter the sex trade profession due to a lack of structural and social network-based interventions put themselves at a greater risk for transphobic violence and murders. The degree to which the black transgender women interviewed who work in this profession expressed their fear of transphobic violence and murders varied, but the most consistent responses were that the doers of the majority of these heinous violence acts was repeatedly black cisgender men. They believed that such violence was based solely on their gender identity due to a form of toxic masculinity. Moreover, they believed that harassment and sexual assault from law enforcement officers worsened their circumstances.

When asked to compare the difference between black cisgender men and white cisgender men, the women reported that the interracial victimization experienced by white cisgender men was more of an assault on their race and gender identity through verbal abuse, physical violence, and some sexual violence. In comparison, the intraracial victimization by black cisgender men included more sexual violence and the possibility of death due to the toxic masculinity embedded in the black patriarchal culture. According to Mia Ryan, in her description of the victimization experienced by transgender sex workers:

> When I worked these streets, I was more afraid of black cis men than white cis men. When I serviced white cis men, most were nice to me. Those who did talk shit to me, I didn't know if it was just them being a racist asshole who wanted a black trans woman who they saw as both a man and woman to be submissive to them or not. But on the other hand, when black cis men talked shit, it meant their masculinity was working in the reverse. I could see the wheels [in their mind] turning like 'What am I doing?' or 'What have I done?'

I will say that the longer you're in the game you learn the tricks of the trade. Before I stopped, I only solicited higher clientele to avoid the violence but there's no full-proof method.

Alexandria Sweet in her response also explained the divergent nature of black cisgender men and white cisgender men:

It's crazy because both cis men, black and white, treat us like we aren't human. White men sometimes treat us as endangered species. They almost treat us like delicate animals that need to be nurtured and then conquered. Before and after sex, they're nurturing. But during sex, they're aggressive. To compare, black men treat us like property. We're their property to use us any way they see fit. They're aggressive from start to finish.

Most of the white ones like black trans women who are barely passable. A guy told me once, 'You look too much like a woman, I can't do to you what I want.' The black ones like passable.

Bobbie Golden offered the following sentiment when discussing her fear of black cisgender men and mistreatment from law enforcement officers:

It's sad when you have to worry about your own kind killing you more than the white man. To top it off, when you go to the police for help it's always a black one who gives you the most shit. When they say to you after you ask for help, 'Let me pat you down to see if you're carrying a weapon.' Pat me down, huh? Frisk me, huh? He tryin' to feel that bulge, but won't admit it.

The black transgender women believed that the harassment and sexual assault from law enforcement officers also make it difficult for them to participate safely in the sex trade profession. On the one hand, the women acknowledged that they participate in an illegal business in which they lobbied should be decriminalized.[56] Instead of criminalizing them, they believed that it was important to abolish the systems of oppression that deny employment opportunities due to their gender identity as transgender. On the other hand, the women argued that the actions of the law enforcement officers run counter to their responsibility to serve and protect. Such unethical sexual behavior toward sex workers, in general, has been a problem for decades. However, this police malfeasance toward transgender sex workers is more problematic due to the patriarchal ways in which they perform their job. According to Sophie Rush, "I've went through it all from illegal body search to calling me by my government name. They'll misgender you or call you by the wrong pronoun in a minute to let you know who's in control. These cops don't give a fuck."

Many of the women believed that they could not use any form of legal channels to file a complaint against a law enforcement officer because it often works against them leading to sex work-related arrest. Alexandria Sweet explained that, "The first time I went to jail was when I threatened a black cop that I'd report him. He called my bluff and took my ass to jail." Venus Love described a similar encounter with a law enforcement officer, "One of these niggas sucker punched me one day when negotiating. He didn't like my prices. I saw a [black] cop and told him I'd been assaulted. His response was, 'You need your ass kicked for dressing like a woman.'"

Others expressing similar views as Venus maintained that law enforcement officers struggle to contain this epidemic within the black community due to a dereliction of duty. A transgender sex worker, for example, will have to deal with a law enforcement officers victimizing them or revictimizing them (Stotzer 2009). Venus expressed firmly that, "After that incident, I was finished with cops. When I've feared for my life [since then], I chose not to go to them for help." The women frequently mentioned that within the black community where most of them work, they generally believed that the black law enforcement officers were not sympathetic to the transphobic violence and murders against black transgender women. Venus concluded by indicating, "White cop, black cop, it doesn't matter. It's just disappointing when the black cop doesn't even try to help."

Toxic Masculinity in the Sex Trade Profession

The next stage to trying to understand the complex dynamic between black cisgender men, who are said to commit these transphobic acts of violence and murders, and black transgender women, who participate in the sex trade profession, was to discover how their lives meet head-on in a violent manner. It is established that transgender people who identify with a certain race are more likely to habitat in communities of the same race and socioeconomic status.[57] This information allows us to definitively know that intra-racial violence and murders are a part of the equation within the black community.[58] Despite the predictive validity of this, there is also a need to identify the ways in which they meet, the negotiation of the sex trade, and the toxic masculine effect after the sex act that all have implications for informing us how this powerful form of masculinity claims the lives of black transgender women.

The women interviewed provided a basic rationale for understanding this prevailing problem. For example, Sophie Rush explained that, in general, more transgender women have stopped working as street-level sex workers and advertise on the social media platforms of Backpage.com, Tumblr.com, Plenty of Fish (Pof.com), Instagram.com, and Snapchat.com.[59] "I quit walking the streets a long time ago. I prefer Backpage.com. I know girls who use all of them. These websites give us a certain level of protection. I'm not saying that they keep us totally safe, but it helps," according to Sophie. Table 3.1 provides samples of escort advertisements from Backpage.com to illustrate how these women solicit paid sex. From the samples in the table, we see that these women specify their race, age, type of call (in-call or out-call), and provide a description of the type of services they offer to clients. Most advertisements show that the clients will be paying with donations or contribution, which serves as legal protection and is code for monetary exchange of sexual acts and services.

Table 3.1. Samples of Escort Advertisements from Backpage.com.

Race	Age	Type of Call – In/Out	Descriptions of Escort Advertisement
Latina	21	Both	Hey Guys I'm _____ with a little bit of sugar and a whole lot of spice. [emoji] I have a fun, open-minded and friendly personality. [emoji] I guarantee that you will want to see me again and again. By contacting me you agree to donation being for my time and companionship and that you are not part of ANY law enforcement.
Black	22	Both	Hey fellas im _____ a black sexy slim fully functional hung lady boy for you guys to enjoy i am very pleasent very in touch with my sexuality therefore i know how to get myself and a man off im 5/6 120 lbs. 8 & 1/2 inches of cut chocolate and a ball of fun i provide a very quiet discreet and upscale area and i am looking to host serious inquiries only respond
Black	23	Both	Hi guys I've been gone for a minute now im back to regain my title. I see a lot of new clowns but im the real deal new and improved. If you've seen me before then you know im a beautiful HUNG SHEMALE!! Cant wait to see you xoxoxo!!No block calls serious gentleman only. available now!!! If youre ready to party call me. No black men.

Race	Age	Type of Call – In/Out	Descriptions of Escort Advertisement
Mixed	24	Both	Hello Fellas. My Name Is [name] cute, sexy, passable and very experienced. I aim to please & nothing less [kiss emoji] .soft skin.pretty face pretty hair & nice body. noinappropriate pics.gentlemen with respect only. txt & calls. no private calls. I don't send pics … No African Americans. [phone number]. No Cheap People.serious people only
Black	26	Both	Do you have a boring love life? Take a walk on the wild side with me, while no one is watching! 5'11 HUGE Boobs 38DDD's and 9 1/2" FULLY Functional she-Treat
Black	26	Both	Discreet freak sweaty activity versatile big dick CD love to eat booty love to be on top love to receive if you looking for a freak call me kinky blue I know just what you need my legs stay open my cogk stays hard and my lips stay freaky so if you can handle so if you cool with that hit me up let's make some magic happen in car or My place or outcalls available 24 hours
Black	27	Both	10 fully functional secret! Domination ** Fetishes ** Role playing ECT. [emoji] PARTYTIME !!!! [emoji] Available for kind, mature gentlemen [emoji] Professional & Discreet Companionship Provided [emoji] Non-Rushed fun filled time spent with me [emoji] I Always Work Alone One On One Service [emoji] I CATER TO ALL NEEDS FOR YOU ANACONDA LOVERS!!!!10ACTUAL SIZE!!!! Shemale Meat hit me up [phone number] [name]
Black	29	Both	[phone number] the best. Text me. hung sexy an verse whatever you like no black guys accepted I like white boys
Black	34	Both	im 5.7 140 34 c breast size 9 tasty inches call me [phone number] i,m top an bottom whichever you like. safe location no black guys

(Continued)

Table 3.1. (*Continued*)

Race	Age	Type of Call – In/Out	Descriptions of Escort Advertisement
Mixed	44	Both	NO NO NO NO NO NO TEXTING PLZ READ NO TEXTING. I CANT RECEIVE THEM. MATURE WHITE OLDER MEN ONLY WHITE GENTLEMAN ONLY !!! NO OTHER RACES!!!!!! WHEN CALLING PLZ BE VERY DIRECT, (BLUNT) AND TO THE POINT OF YOUR INTEREST OF YOUR VISIT. NO BS AND AND NO 1ST TIMERS

Source: http://backpage.com
Note: The title of the post is not provided in an effort to protect the identities of the women. The descriptions are provided as-is from the advertisements.

A review of the escort advertisements from Backpage.com shows that a lot of the women, regardless of race and ethnicity, will include a line in the description of their services that forbids black cisgender men from contacting them. Some will post a photo on their page with the words "No African-Americans." Relying on these advertisements to begin a multistage descriptive analysis, it is clear that most transgender women would prefer not to service these men. According to Alexandria Sweet, "It's no secret anymore, [black] cis men are acting violently toward us. As a trans woman, each and every day I fear for my life. I've been sexually and physically assaulted. The same thing has happened to my friends as well." After identifying the frequency of each advertisement that read either, "No Black Men," "No African-Americans," or "Black Men 35+ only," the next step was to contact these women to gauge the seriousness of their advertisements.

From the counsel of Sophie Rush, she advised that the best approach would be to contact women from Backpage.com and present both an urban dialect and polite dialect to ascertain whether these women would service black cisgender men. Sophie articulated, "I suggest you just call them and see what type of business they're doing. Call first and sound urban as hell and call again sounding like Carlton [from the Fresh Prince of Bel-Air].[60] I bet you get a different reaction." While this exercise is not applicable to a violent motive, it does allow the ability to establish profiles of individuals who these women were less likely to service. According to Mia Ryan, "In most cases with phone calls, they are methods to filter black men. That's why the younger girls use other social media to see who they are communicating with. This eases their fears. They may put 'upscale gentlemen only' in their profile but they can't control who contacts them.[61] Some black men will just call to vent about you not accepting black men."

The scripts were as follows:

- Script: Urban Dialect—What's up shorty, my name is _____. Are you available to meet today? [pause for response] I'm a black dude. I see your profile says 'no black dudes.' [wait on her to respond]
- Script: Polite Dialect—Hello _____, my name is _____. Are you available to meet today? I'm in town on a business trip and leave tomorrow. [pause for response] I would like to tell you up front that I'm a black man. [wait on her to respond]

Table 3.2 shows the results from the two hypothetical scripts of the pre-post inquiry. Prior to this exercise, I, as well as Sophie, expected that younger transgender sex workers would be more lenient in their stance than older transgender sex workers. Specifically, younger transgender sex workers would be more likely to change their position in spite of hearing the urban dialect. Conversely, older transgender sex workers would be steadfast in their position. The table showed that the results were mixed. A significant number of those who listed either, "No Black Men," or "No African-Americans" on their advertisements, regardless of age, continued to reject black men as clients with an urban dialect. Only a small percentage of these women were willing to accept black men with a proper dialect (see Table 3.2). In other words, the table appears to be representative of the claim that black transgender women were less likely to service black cisgender men. In developing a theorem, we cannot say based on the calls that it is because these men present a higher probability of danger to these women. It could be the case that this small, convenient sample size is skewed.

The next stage of understanding the risk assessment led to questions about the negotiation of the sex trade and the toxic masculine effect after the sex act. According to Bobbie Golden:

> Negotiating with these motherfuckers is the worse. I always want to know [but don't always ask]: Are you a first-timer? Are you experimenting? Are you a tranny-chaser? Do you think we are freaks and you want to fuck a freak? Do you want to see my dick when we are fucking? Do you not want to see my dick when we are fucking? Do you consider yourself straight? After we fuck, do you want to forget it ever happened? Do you want me to leave the [hotel] room first? Do you want to leave [the hotel room] first? If we could put these questions on an application, it would help protect us. Trust me.

Table 3.2: Pre-Post Phone Inquiry.

Race	Age	Type of Call – In/Out	Accept Black Men on Advertisement	Accept Black Men after Call Inquiry (*Urban Dialect*)	Accept Black Men after Call Inquiry (*Proper Dialect*)
Mixed	24	Both	No	No	Yes
Black	24	Both	No	No	Yes
White	27	Both	No	No	No
Mixed	19	Both	No	Yes	Yes
Black	28	Both	No	No	Yes
Mexican	26	Both	No	Yes	Yes
White	36	In	No	No	No
White	25	Both	No	No	No
Black	18	Both	No	Yes	Yes
Black	25	Both	No	No	No
Black	23	Both	No	Yes	Yes
Black	26	Both	No	No	Yes
Asian	23	Out	No	No	No
Black	22	Both	No	Yes	Yes
Mexican/White	29	In	No	No	No
Mexican	27	In	No	No	Yes
Asian	41	Both	No	No	No
Black	24	Both	No	No	No
Mixed	27	Both	No	No	No
Mexican	32	Both	No	No	No
Mexican	25	Both	No	No	No
White	28	Both	No	No	No
Mexican	32	Both	No	No	No
Black	24	Both	No	No	No
Black	22	Both	No	Yes	Yes
Mexican	26	Both	No	No	No
Black	22	Both	No	Yes	Yes
Mexican	25	Both	No	No	No
No Picture	33	Both	No	No	No
Mexican	22	Both	No	Yes	Yes
Mexican	24	Both	No	No	No
Black	33	Both	No	No	No
White	25	Both	No	No	No
Black	22	Both	No	Yes	Yes
Mexican	25	Both	No	No	No

Race	Age	Type of Call – In/Out	Accept Black Men on Advertisement	Accept Black Men after Call Inquiry (*Urban Dialect*)	Accept Black Men after Call Inquiry (*Proper Dialect*)
Black	30	Both	No	No	No
Mexican	22	Both	No	No	Yes
Hispanic	27	Both	No	No	No
Black	34	Both	No	No	No
Black	28	Both	No	No	No
Black	24	Both	No	No	Yes
Mexican	28	Both	No	No	No
Black	26	Both	No	No	No
Mexican	24	Both	No	No	No
Mexican	22	Both	No	No	Yes
Mexican	28	Both	No	No	No
White	21	Both	No	Yes	Yes
Mexican	19	Both	No	No	No
Black	23	Both	No	No	No
Black	20	Both	No	Yes	Yes

Source: http://houston.backpage.com/TranssexualEscorts
Notes: (a) This descriptive table contains the first fifty transgender women profiles posted under a Houston Backpage.com transsexual escorts page from January 1–5, 2016. Those listed indicated that they do not provide services to black men as clients. Repeats during this time frame were not included. (b) Each of the transgender sex workers was called with a prepaid cell phone to inquire whether they would accept black male clients regardless of their advertisement. (c) A similar exercise was performed with white cisgender men. There was little to no variation. (d) There were advertisements that accepted black men as clients over 35-years-old. Those were excluded.

> I think everyone you interview [of the black transgender women] will tell you the same thing, most of these black men have to get high to fuck us. After we've gone through the bullshit of trying to only service black men who won't fuck over us, we find out that either they are high as hell and that gives them courage [to be with us] or their high will lead to them acting out.

Most of the black transgender women interviewed agreed that the negotiation of the sex trade is often a preliminary assessment of the risks associated with servicing a client. Venus Love specified in her response that the lack of knowledge of how to solicit a transgender sex worker builds inner masculine tension:

It's the first sign [of a situation becoming violent] because they don't know what to ask for and the cost associated with it. Negotiating with us is not like negotiating with a cis woman. If they're a first-timer, they should be negotiating for time and not a particular sex act. The back and forth negotiation builds tension.

Some of them want to see us naked before they agree to pay us which really means that they want to see the size of our penis. If they're into that, fine. But if they're not into that, the bigger our penis the less of a man they feel like.

Venus's position spoke to a certain etiquette that black cisgender men should practice when soliciting transgender sex workers. As most of the women agreed, trying to negotiate down the price and bidding to receive multiple sex acts for less money creates an unpredictable atmosphere. Alexandria Sweet pointed out that:

When negotiations don't work in their favor, they begin to talk really aggressive. They talk to us like we're men. And I'll be honest, most of us haven't taken hormones for a very long time so our voices do have some bass in them. When we get mad and have to defend ourselves, our voices get loud.

Last week I had someone pull out his penis as soon as we got into the hotel room. I ended up walking out. When things like that happen, it's not good. When they want you to go straight to business with no pay, I avoid those every time.

By far the most common precaution when negotiating was "to stay close to the door" to exit in case of danger. The women, for the most part, believed that staying close to the door was a safey precaution to avoid being beaten or raped when negotiations failed. According to Sophie Rush, "I'm old school, I used to stay close to the door and carry a little something in my purse. Back then I carried a whistle and a gun."

When discussing the violence and murders toward them, all agreed that a toxic form of masculinity emerges after the sex act. Naomi Mars made clear, "We can't hang around afterwards like others [cisgender sex workers] unless it's a client we know very well. From the time he [is relieved], to you getting dressed and leaving is crucial. He'll come down from that high or drunk and fuck you up!" Sophie Rush echoed a similar thought, "These black cis boys are paying for anonymity. It's not like being with a white boy who is rich, has a family, and only wants a prostitute for just sex with no strings attached. The black ones want that but they also want to walk away with their masculinity intact. After he gets his, you need to be careful." Naomi went on to say that, "After they [are relieved] I hurry up and put on my clothes and get the fuck out of dodge."

The black transgender women's perception of toxic masculinity was consistent with understanding that it is a violent form of masculinity used by cisgender men to prove their manhood. They believed that the tightrope of heteronormativity that these men walk in front of the outside world is conflictual to their masculine persona. Venus Love stressed the need for black cisgender men who commit such violence to "seek help and stop feeling like they have to prove how hard they are. Their fragile egos are going to lead to the deaths of more black trans women." Most of the women believed that black cisgender men look at them one way, which is "for sex purposes only." According to Bobbie Golden, "Once the sex is over, he'll try to make sense of what just happened. If he can't, the shame will take over. Then the verbal abuse will start. He'll do anything to prove how powerful he is over you. That's why it's necessary for me to be on my Ps and Qs."

When women were asked about remaining in the sex trade profession, they exhibited a range of emotions and responses regarding their continuation. While most have temporarily settled for this profession due to "no other employment skills," others are in the process of life changes. According to Naomi Mars, "This has to end. I can't keep putting my life in danger." Naomi, like the other women interviewed in the sex trade profession, explained that they have experienced more than their fair share of violence. They face the future optimistically believing that this "means of economic survival" will not ultimately be the death of them and wanting to participate in social service programs to leave the profession.

Conclusion

This chapter has called for a clearer understanding of the comorbidity of race and gender identity bias that makes black transgender women most susceptible to transphobic violence and murders. When applying a micro-level and macro-level intersectional approach to explore the situational and cultural contexts that foster such violence, it was evident that these survivors of hate-based violence, intimate partner violence, and sex work related violence all suffer from the intersectional identities and interlocking systems of oppression that enable these forms of structural and cultural violence. We have established that the constructs of race, gender identity, and socioeconomic status operate as distinct identity signifiers. These oppressive constructs, along with the authoritative power of patriarchy, feed a societal and cultural epidemic that disproportionately affects black transgender women.

The continued peeling back of the layers of their lived experiences show that these women are confronted with a serious set of violent outcomes. Their narratives help to corroborate the claim that situational and cultural contexts by and large play a central role in grasping how they are exposed to such violence. From their responses, we further learn that a patriarchal system of male domination breeds gender-based oppression that violently challenges the existence of these women through the situational contexts of hate-based violence and intimate partner violence. To maintain a rigid gender order, men of all demographics, perform these toxic acts of violence against transgender women who they believe transgress gender norms.

Within the black community, cultural context is important for the evaluation of risk for violence. The cultural context of intimate partner violence and violence against transgender sex workers poses a growing concern for these women. As discussed in Chapter 2, the women suggest that a set of communal and cultural values is the reason for the heteropatriarchal way of experiencing the perception of gender. Thus, hindering cultural acceptance and inclusion while exacerbating transphobic attitudes and behaviors. When toxic masculinity is added to the cultural context to explain transphobic violence in a black patriarchal culture, the women expressed greater fear of life-threatening violence.

As stated, not all transgender women work in this profession. However, their participation provided substantive input to gain greater insight into a world of sex work-related violence that would otherwise only be seen through a somewhat limited lens with other transgender women. The cultural aspects of this type of work inevitably make these women vulnerable to various forms of structural and cultural violence. The women interviewed indicated that such abuse and violence extends from black cisgender men to law enforcement officers who use their badge and position as a means of control.

In interpreting how violence targets these women in general, Jauk (2013, p. 822) argues that it is of great utility to "refocus on the multidimensionality of violence in transgendered lives and how it plays out along the lines of race, class, and gender." I believe as well that it is equally important not to conflate hate-based violence with other forms of violence in order to accurately explain the impact and effects of the violence against them.[62] Take, for example, the scenarios mentioned in the introduction of this chapter, hate was not the primary motive in all of them but was correlated as such when explaining the violent outcomes. Rather than arguing blindly that these crimes are motivated by hate as the root cause, it is imperative to comprehend what happened, the proper context for it happening, and how to prevent it from happening again. This is the most objective way to address the abuse and violence against black transgender women.

In conclusion, it helps in understanding how black transgender women cope with such traumatic events and the precautions to avoid future reoccurrences. These points are discussed further in Chapter 4, which presents a case study of the life histories of three black transgender women—Sophie Rush, Mia Ryan, and Jessica Sugar—who all detail the complexities of life as a black transgender woman.

Notes

1. See the 2014 recorded interview and obtain the transcript of, "'Black trans bodies are under attack": Freed activist CeCe McDonald, actress Laverne Cox speak out." *DemocracyNow.com*. Available at: https://www.democracynow.org/2014/2/19/black_trans_bodies_are_under_attack (February 19).
2. See Holden, D. 2015. "Evidence contradicts police account of possible anti-transgender hate crime." *Buzzfeed.com*. Available at: https://www.buzzfeed.com/dominicholden/evidence-contradicts-police-account-of-possible-anti-transge?utm_term=.uwwZkw49q4#.bnELexWaAW (March 6).
3. Ibid.
4. Ibid.
5. Ibid.
6. Gleaves was also convicted of tampering with physical evidence (Class D felony). He asked his girlfriend Zsanaza Duffy, 20, to destroy his cell phone.
7. See Smith, L. 2016. "Henry Gleaves sentenced to 7 years on manslaughter, tampering charges." *WDRB.com*. Available at: http://www.wdrb.com/story/32740834/verdict-jury-deliberating-fate-of-accused-murderer-henry-gleaves (August 11).
8. See the 2015 National Coalition of Anti-Violence Programs (NCAVP) report, "NCAVP mourns the death of Lamia Beard, a transgender woman of color killed in Norfolk, Virginia; the first homicide of a transgender woman of color that NCAVP has responded to in 2015." Available at: http://avp.org/storage/documents/1.22.15_ncavp_ma_lamiabeardva.pdf.
9. For more information on the details of the case, see the arrest warrant affidavit. Available at: http://ftpcontent4.worldnow.com/kltv/PDF/underwoodaffidavit.pdf.
10. Ibid.
11. See McCoy, C. 2015. "Carlton Champion Jr. sentenced to life in prison for murder of transgender woman." *TylerPaper.com*. Available at: http://www.tylerpaper.com/TP-News+Local/228569/champion-sentenced-to-life (December 18).
12. See Daley, E. 2015. "College football player sentenced to life for killing Texas trans woman." *Advocate.com*. Available at: http://www.advocate.com/crime/2015/12/18/college-football-player-sentenced-life-killing-texas-transgender-woman (December 18).
13. Ibid.
14. The principal foundation of Crenshaw's analysis was to describe the exclusion of black women from white feminist discourse and antiracist discourse. Intersectionality is not a theory, but rather, a framework to explain a phenomenon.
15. See Lynch (2005, p. 3) who points out that "gender involves identities beyond women and needs to be understood as femininity, masculinity, gender queer, transgender, men, women, and beyond."
16. See Gutierrez-Morfin, N. 2016. "Hate violence against trans people still 'Disturbingly Common'." *NBCNews.com*. Available at: http://www.nbcnews.com/feature/nbc-out/hate-violence-against-trans-people-still-disturbingly-common-n685971 (November 20).
17. Ibid.

18. We should be aware that there is also a group of feminists, TERFs or trans-exclusive radical feminists, who believe that transgender women should not be considered "real women." The most notable is radical feminist activist, blogger, and attorney Cathy Brennan. In 2011, Brennan and a colleague wrote a letter to the United Nations arguing that certain laws prohibiting discrimination based on gender identity and gender expression "undermines legal protections for females vis-a-vis sex segregated spaces." Letter available at: https://genderidentitywatch. files.wordpress.com/2012/09/communication_csw_un_brennanhungerford_08012011_pdf.

19. Under this Act, the U.S. Congress made it a crime to use, or threaten to use, force to interfere with housing rights because of the victim's race, color, religion, sex, or national origin. It does not include sexual orientation, gender, or disability. In 1988, protections related to familial status were added to the Act.

20. See the FBI's Hate Crime Statistics homepage, "About Hate Crime Statistics." Available at: https://ucr.fbi.gov/hate-crime/2010/resources/hate-crime-2010-about-hate-crime.

21. The 2009 Matthew Shepard and James Byrd Jr., Hate Crimes Prevention Act was named after two historic hate crimes. On June 7, 1998, James Byrd Jr., a black American, was lynched-by-dragging. Three white men in Jasper, Texas dragged him behind a pick-up truck severing his arm and head. Months later, Matthew Wayne Shepard, a gay man, was beaten and tortured due to his sexual orientation. In 2016, this Act was utilized in the case of Joshua Vallum who murdered Mercedes Williamson, a transgender teenager. For a full description of the Act, visit the U.S. Department of Justice website. Available at: https://www.justice. gov/crt/matthew-shepard-and-james-byrd-jr-hate-crimes-prevention-act-2009-0.

22. See Bronski, M., Pellegrini, A., and M. Amico. 2013. "Hate crime laws don't prevent violence against LGBT people." *TheNation.com*. Available at: https://www.thenation.com/ article/hate-crime-laws-dont-prevent-violence-against-lgbt-people (October 2).

23. See the FBI's Hate Crime Statistics, "Hate Crime Statistics, 2013." Available at: https://ucr. fbi.gov/hate-crime/2013/topic-pages/incidents-and-offenses/incidentsandoffenses_final.

24. The breakdown is 23 anti-transgender and eight anti-gender non-conforming.

25. FBI's Hate Crime Statistics, Hate Crime Statistics, 2013

26. The findings from this NCAVP report titled, "Lesbian, gay, bisexual, transgender, queer and HIV-affected hate violence in 2012" has been challenged because it counts some cases not classified as crimes by law enforcement officials. Full report available at: http://www. avp.org/storage/documents/2013_ncavp_hvreport_final.pdf

27. Ibid.

28. See Michaels, S. 2015. "It's incredibly scary to be a transgender woman of color right now." *MotherJones.com*. Available at: http://www.motherjones.com/politics/2015/06/transgender-women-disproportionately-targeted-violent-hate-crimes (June 26).

29. See the FBI's Hate Crime Statistics, "Hate Crime Statistics, 2014." Available at: https:// ucr.fbi.gov/about-us/cjis/ucr/hate-crime/2014/topic-pages/victims_final.

30. Lee and Kwan (2014, p. 95) note that prior to this Act, "hate crimes against transgender individuals may be significantly underreported because gender identity bias is often mischaracterized as bias on the basis of sexual orientation."

31. See Cassidy, C. A. 2016. "Patchy reporting undercuts national hate crimes count." *AP.org*. Available at: http://bigstory.ap.org/article/8247a1d2f76b4baea2a121186dedf768/ ap-patchy-reporting-undercuts-national-hate-crimes-count (June 5).

32. See the 2016 Human Rights Campaign (HRC) article, "Human rights campaign statement on tragic shooting at Orlando nightclub serving LGBTQ community." Available at: http://www.hrc.org/blog/human-rights-campaign-statement-on-tragic-shooting-at-orlando-nightclub-ser (June 12).

33. In a 2016 60 Minute interview following the rise of hate-based violence, President-elect Donald J. Trump looked into the camera and said to the aggressors of these crimes, "If it helps, I will say this, and I will say right to the cameras: Stop it." See ABC News (2016, November 14). *Trump Calls for Hate Crimes to Stop* [Video File]. Available at: https://www.youtube.com/watch?v=WDM5EWieJzg.

34. For the full 2016 Southern Poverty Law Center (SPLC) report titled, "Ten days after: Harassment and intimidation in the aftermath of the election," is available at: https://www.splcenter.org/sites/default/files/com_hate_incidents_report_final.pdf.

35. Ibid.

36. It is also important to note that reports surfaced following the presidential election that indicated transgender people were in favor of detransitioning to avoid hate-based violence. In an online poll, 36% of transgender people "said they'd decided to detransition or were seriously considering it after the election." For more information, see the 2016 *Huffington Post* article titled, "The trans people who are detransitioning to stay safe in Trump's America." Available at: http://www.huffingtonpost.com/entry/the-trans-people-who-are-detransitioning-to-stay-safe_us_5840bb7ce4b04587de5de897?section=us_queer-voices& (December 1).

37. For a full report, see James, S. E., Herman, J. L., Rankin, S., Keisling, M., Mottet, L., and M. Ana. 2016. *Executive Summary of the Report of the 2015 U.S. Transgender Survey.* Washington, DC: National Center for Transgender Equality. Available at: http://www.transequality.org/sites/default/files/docs/USTS-Executive-Summary-FINAL.PDF.

38. Whitlock (2001, p. 8), in a booklet titled, "In a time of broken bones" called for more dialogue on hate-based crime and legislation to address it. She argues that, "Attempting to address hate violence in ways that reinforce the structural violence of this system will only fuel the cycle of violence, hatred, and polarization." The booklet is available at: https://www.afsc.org/sites/afsc.civicactions.net/files/documents/In_A_Time_Of_Broken_Bones.pdf.

39. See Comstock (1991) in his seminal research of violence against lesbians and gay men for a similar view. This research found that mostly heterosexual men have committed violence against LGBTQ people and it has been random and brutal.

40. Lee and Kwan (2014, p. 98) define provocation as "a partial defense, not a complete defense, because the defendant who successfully argues provocation is not fully absolved of criminal liability. The defendant is merely acquitted of the charged offense but convicted of a lesser offense."

41. Visiting the http://www.rememberingourdead.org will lead to the following statement "The original 'Remembering Our Dead Project' is, unfortunately, not still visible at either its original site nor at The Internet Archive." This quote was obtained and confirmed from multiple secondary sources.

42. See Chibbaro, L. 2015. "Police: Trans woman killed after suspect 'embarrassed.'" *WashingtonBlade.com*. Available at: http://www.washingtonblade.com/2015/10/18/police-trans-woman-killed-after-suspect-embarrassed (October 18).

43. Human Rights Campaign (HRC), Human rights campaign statement on tragic shooting at Orlando nightclub serving LGBTQ community

44. See the Centers for Disease Control and Prevention website for their full-length description of intimate partner violence. Available at: https://www.cdc.gov/violenceprevention/intimatepartnerviolence/definitions.html.

45. See the 2013 Bureau of Justice Statistics (BLS) report, "Intimate partner violence: Attributes of victimization, 1993–2011." Available at: http://www.bjs.gov/index.cfm?ty=pbdetail&iid=4801.

46. James et al., Executive Summary of the Report of the 2015 U.S. Transgender Survey

47. See Brown, T. N. T., and J. L. Herman. 2015. "Intimate partner violence and sexual abuse among LGBT people: A review of existing literature." *The Williams Institute*. Available at: http://williamsinstitute.law.ucla.edu/wp-content/uploads/Intimate-Partner-Violence-and-Sexual-Abuse-among-LGBT-People.pdf.

48. Ibid.

49. A full description of the 2011 report conducted by the National Gay and Lesbian Task Force and the National Center for Transgender Equality (NCTE), "Injustice at every turn: A report of the national transgender discrimination survey," can be found at: http://www.thetaskforce.org/static_html/downloads/reports/reports/ntds_full.pdf.

50. Ibid.

51. Ibid.

52. A full description of the 2015 report, "Meaningful work: Transgender experiences in the sex trade," conducted by the National Center for Transgender Equality (NCTE), the Red Umbrella Project (RedUP), and Best Practices Policy Project (BPPP), can be found at: http://www.transequality.org/sites/default/files/Meaningful%20Work-Full%20Report_FINAL_3.pdf.

53. James et al., Executive Summary of the Report of the 2015 U.S. Transgender Survey

54. See Wilson et al. (2009) who provide an excellent analysis on transgender female youth (15–24) and sex work. They explore the life factors associated with entering the sex trade profession.

55. James et al., Executive Summary of the Report of the 2015 U.S. Transgender Survey

56. See Weitzer (2012) for a comprehensive discussion on the legalization of sex work.

57. See Flores, A. R., Brown, T. N. T., and J. L. Herman. 2016. "Race and ethnicity of adults who identify as transgender in the United States." *The Williams Institute*. Available at: http://williamsinstitute.law.ucla.edu/wp-content/uploads/Race-and-Ethnicity-of-Transgender-Identified-Adults-in-the-US.pdf.

58. See Wilson (2009) for an in-depth analysis of structural and cultural factors within the black community. For a thorough review on cultural factors that impact black males, see Orlando Patterson, "Taking Culture Seriously: A Framework and an Afro-American Illustration," In L. E. Harrison and S. P. Huntington (Eds.), *Culture matters: How values shape human progress* (New York: Basic Books, 2000), pp. 202–218.

59. On January 9, 2017, Backpage.com closed its online adult advertising section in the USA. This decision came before their founders, Michael Lacey and James Larkin, and the site's CEO, Carl Ferrer, were scheduled to testify before the U.S. Congress related to withheld evidence on sex work and child sex trafficking. Backpage.com was said to have edited up

to 80% of such advertisements to maintain them on their website. On their website (Backpage.com), it reads that, "The government has unconstitutionally censored this content." In a phone call with Sophie Rush on the day of the decision, she believed that, "this will force more black trans girls to walk the streets. Watch the murders increase. Some will just move their ads to the 'dating t >' label, which will definitely increase violence because men will feel deceived. For the most part, it's not good for business."

60. The reference to "Carlton Banks" played by actor, Alfonso L. Ribeiro Sr., symbolizes a pejorative phase for 'acting white.' On the television show, Carlton is an intelligent, conservative Republican black man who speaks with proper dialect.

61. It should be noted that some of the women interviewed mentioned advertising on Eros.com (or Erostranssexuals.com), which is known as an upscale escort website that serves professional men. None chose to advertise on the website due to the expensive advertising cost, restrictions on the wording of their advertisements, and limited anonymity. In January of 2017, there was only one black transgender woman soliciting in the Houston Trans section of the website.

62. This claim is also supported by several other studies. See, for example, Goodmark (2012)

References

Anthias, F. 2013. Intersectionality what? Social divisions, intersectionality and levels of analysis. *Ethnicities* 13(1): 3–19.

Beale, F. 1970. Double jeopardy: To be black and female. In T. Cade (Ed.), *The black woman: An anthology* (90–110). New York: Signet.

Bond, J. C., and P. Perry. 1970. Is the Black Male castrated? In T. Cade (Ed.), *The black woman: An anthology* (113–118). New York: Signet.

Bowleg, L. 2012. The problem with the phrase *women and minorities*: Intersectionality—an important theoretical framework for public health. *American Journal of Public Health* 102(7): 1267–1273.

Buist, C. L., and C. Stone. 2014. Transgender victims and offenders: Failures of the United States criminal justice system and the necessity of queer criminology. *Critical Criminology* 22(1): 35–47.

Collins, P. H. 1990. *Black feminist thought: Knowledge, consciousness, and the politics of empowerment.* Boston: Unwin Hyman.

Collins, P. H. 2000. *Black feminist thought: Knowledge, consciousness, and the politics of empowerment, 2nd Edition.* New York: Routledge.

Collins, P. H. 2003. Some group matters: Intersectionality, situated standpoints, and black feminist thought. In T. L. Lott and J. P. Pittman (Eds.), *A companion to African-American philosophy* (205–229). Oxford: Blackwell.

Collins, P. H. 2004. *Black sexual politics: African Americans, gender, and the new racism.* New York: Routledge.

Collins, P. H., Maldonado, L. A., Takagi, D. Y., Thorne, B., Weber, L., and H. Winant. 1995. Symposium on West and Fernmaker's 'Doing Difference.' *Gender and Society* 9(4): 491–513.

Comstock, G. D. 1991. *Violence against lesbians and gay men.* New York: Columbia University Press.

Crenshaw, K. 1989. Demarginalizing the intersection of race and sex: A black feminist critique of antidiscrimination doctrine, feminist theory and antiracist politics. *University of Chicago Legal Forum* 1(8): 139–167.

Crenshaw, K. 1991. Mapping the margins: Intersectionality, identity politics, and violence against women of color. *Stanford Law Review* 43(6): 1241–1299.

Davis, K. 2008. Intersectionality as buzzword: A sociology of science perspective on what makes a feminist theory successful. *Feminist Theory* 9(1): 67–85.

de Vries, K. M. 2012. Intersectional identities and conceptions of the self: The experience of transgender people. *Symbolic Interaction* 35(1): 49–67.

de Vries, K. M. 2014. Transgender people of color at the center: Conceptualizing a new intersectional model. *Ethnicities* 15(1): 1–25.

Drake, D. S. 2004. Confronting and managing GLBT homicide and its associated phenomena. In W. Swan (Ed.), *Handbook of Gay, Lesbian, Bisexual, and Transgender Administration and Policy* (311–348). New York: Marcel Dekker.

Edwards, K. M., Sylaska, K. M., and A. M. Neal. 2015. Intimate partner violence among sexual minority populations: A critical review of the literature and agenda for future research. *Psychology of Violence* 5(2): 112–121.

Goodmark, L. 2012. Transgender people, intimate partner abuse, and the legal system. *Harvard Civil Rights-Civil Liberties Law Review* 48: 51–104.

Greenberg, K. 2012. Still hidden in the closet: Trans women and domestic violence. *27 Berkeley Journal of Gender Law and Justice* 27(2): 198–251.

Guidroz, K., and M. T. Berger. 2010. A Conversation with founding scholars of Intersectionality—Kimberle Crenshaw, Nira Yuval-Davis, and Michelle Fine. In K. Guidroz and M. T. Berger (Eds.), *The intersectional approach: Transforming the academy through race, class, and gender* (61–80). Chapel Hill: The University of North Carolina Press.

hooks, b. 2000. *Feminist theory: From margin to center.* Cambridge, MA: South End Press.

hooks, b. 2004. *The will to change: Men, masculinity, and love.* New York: Washington Square Press.

Jauk, D. 2013. Gender violence revisited: Lessons from violent victimization of transgender identified individuals. *Sexualities* 16(7): 807–825.

Kelley, K., and J. Gruenewald. 2014. Accomplishing masculinity through anti-lesbian, gay, bisexual, and transgender homicide: A comparative case study approach. *Men and Masculinities* 18(1): 3–29.

King, D. 1988. Multiple jeopardy, multiple consciousness: The context of a black feminist ideology. *Signs: Journal of Women in Culture and Society* 14(1): 42–72.

Lee, C., and P. K. Y. Kwan. 2014. The trans panic defense: Heteronormativity, and the murder of transgender women. *66 Hastings L. J. 77*; GWU Law School Public Law Research Paper No. 2014–10; GWU Legal Studies Research Paper No. 2014–10.

Lynch, A. M. 2005. Hate crime as a tool of the gender border patrol: The importance of gender as a protected category. Presented at "When Women Gain, So does the World," IWPR's *Eighth International Women's Policy Research Conference.* Washington, DC, June 19–21.

Meyer, D. 2010. Evaluating the severity of hate-motivated violence: Intersectional differences among LGBT hate crime victims. *Sociology* 44(5): 980–995.

Operario, D., Soma, T., and K. Underhill. 2008. Sex work and HIV status among transgender women: Systemic review and meta-analysis. *The Journal of Acquired Immune Deficiency Syndromes* 48(1): 97–103.

Patil, V. 2013. From patriarchy to intersectionality: A transnational feminist assessment of how far we've really come. *Signs: Journal of Women in Culture and Society* 38(4): 847–867.

Perry, B. 2001. *In the name of hate: Understanding hate crimes.* New York: Routledge.

Perry, B. 2003. Where do we go from here? Researching hate crime. *Internet Journal of Criminology* [Online]. Available at: http://www.internetjournalofcriminology.com/where%20do%20we%20go%20from%20here.%20researching%20hate%20crime.pdf.

Rahman, M. 2010. Queer as intersectionality: Theorizing gay Muslim identities. *Sociology* 44(5): 944–961.

Ruiz-Perez, I., Plazaola-Castano, J., and C. Vives-Cases. 2007. Methodological issues in the study of violence against women. *Journal of Epidemiology and Community Health* 61(2): 26–31.

Sevelius, J. M. 2013. Gender affirmation: A framework for conceptualizing risk behavior among transgender women of color. *Sex Roles* 68(11–12): 675–689.

Smyth, M., and V. Jenness. 2014. Violence against sexual and gender minorities. In R. Gartner, and B. McCarthy (Eds.), *The Oxford Handbook of Gender, Sex, and Crime* (403–423). New York: Oxford University Press.

Stotzer, R. L. 2009. Violence against transgender people: A review of United States data. *Aggression and Violent Behavior* 14(3): 170–179.

Testa, R. J., Sciacca, L. M., Wang, F., Hendricks, M. L., Goldblum, P., Bradford, J., and B. Bonga. 2012. Effects of violence on transgender people. *Professional Psychology: Research and Practice* 43(5): 452–459.

Weitzer, R. 2012. *Legalizing prostitution: From illicit vice to lawful business*. New York: New York University Press.

Whitlock, K. 2001. *In a time of broken bones: A call to dialogue on hate violence and the limitations of hate crimes legislation*. Haverford: American Friends Service Committee.

Wilson, W. J. 2009. *More than just race: Being black and poor in the inner city*. New York: W. W. Norton & Company.

Wilson, E. C., Garofalo, R., Harris, R. D., Herrick, A., Martinez, M., Martinez, J., and M. Belzer. 2009. Transgender female youth and sex work: HIV risk and a comparison of life factors related to engagement in sex work. *AIDS and Behavior* 13(5): 902–913.

Witten, T. M., and A. E. Eyler. 1997. HIV, AIDS and the elderly transgendered/transsexual: Risk and invisibility. Presentation at the Gerontological Society of America, Cincinnati, OH.

Witten, T. M., and A. E. Eyler. 1999. Hate crimes and violence against the transgendered. *Peace Review* 11(3): 461–468.

· 4 ·

BLACK TRANS VOICES

Their Lived Experiences

No one but trans women has any idea how hard our lives can be after we come out. I mean this was a difficult choice to make because I knew there would be significant consequences. I still have yet to deal with some of the consequences of my decision.
—Sophie Rush

What does it mean to be a black transgender woman within the black community and in the larger American society? This chapter seeks to get to the heart of this question by giving three black transgender women—Sophie Rush, Mia Ryan, and Jessica Sugar—an opportunity to provide extensive knowledge about their lived experiences. Given that the voice of this understudied group has mainly been muted in the landscape of American society, this chapter hopes to capture an accurate snapshot of the life histories of these women through participant observations and in-depth interviews.

As noted in the preceding chapters, black transgender women face a myriad of hardships in their lives. According to Meyer (2008, 2010), the lived experiences of black LGBTQIA people, particularly black transgender women, differ significantly from the rest of the larger LGBTQIA community. A chapter that examines the extensive systemic, institutional, and interpersonal circumstances that affect black transgender women through their own eyes is essential to provide a holistic view. The objective is to attempt to unlock the oppressive constructs of race, sexuality, and gender identity, and the socioeconomic status said to exist in the dominant norms of heterosexuality which leads the majority of these women to live on the margins of society; a place, according to Mia Ryan, where "[F]ull inclusion is a façade in our world. It will never happen in my lifetime."

In this chapter, three major themes will be examined: First, "My Born Self," which discusses their evolution from being medically assigned the sex of male at birth to their transition to black transgender women. Second, "I Am a Black Woman, Too," which talks about the heteropatriarchy embedded within the black community and in the larger American society that works to negate the ability of transgender women to be considered "real women." This patriarchal structure supports systems of toxic masculinity, and at times, toxic femininity among black cisgender women. Third and last, "We Need Protection," which allows the women to explain the necessity of protecting black transgender women from transphobic violence and murders. These interrelated themes provide significant insight into the societal and cultural marginalization of black transgender women.

Sophie Rush, 39, Escort

These young black trans girls be "pussy stuntin". That means they won't tell a cis boy they are trans until they are confronted or forced to, which is fucked up. It only works when girls are passable. They operate under a military code, "Don't Ask, Don't Tell." That code is sometimes getting them murdered.

—Sophie Rush

Sophie Rush, at 39 years of age, is the elder stateswoman among the black transgender women. We initially met at a popular donut shop, *Shipley's Do-Nuts*, in the Woodlands area, a majority white, quiet suburban community outside of Houston, Texas. The Woodlands is approximately 28 miles north of the heart of Houston, which led to one of the first questions asked during our scheduled interview, "Why did you want to meet in the Woodlands? I thought you lived off of Westheimer Road."[1] Her response was straightforward, "I only fuck with white boys. They pay well. No drama for me. Plus, it's the holiday season. They love black trans girls for Christmas."

When I arrived at *Shipley's Do-Nuts*, Sophie had set up shop—laptop out and a pen and notepad in front of her—looking like she was ready to conduct business. I asked what was she working on due to the setup of the workspace. "Multiple things," she replied. Sophie once worked in corporate America, and she treated her current profession with the same workwoman-like approach. She was updating her Backpage.com profile and adding new pictures and a video to her Tumblr.com page. When Sophie allowed me to take a look at her Backpage.com profile, several things were readily apparent: *She was drama-free, drug-free, by appointment only, in-calls only, not interested in pimps, and not interested in servicing black men at all.* Sophie explained that at her age it was of great consequence to be as careful as possible.

In her early years in the sex trade profession, she had been raped, gang-raped, and almost beaten to death, all of which she wanted to avoid in the future. She only operates as an escort for two weeks out of the month. In those two weeks, Sophie travels to the Woodlands area to create separation from where she works and resides. She rents a small apartment to suit her white clientele. According to her, "White boys feel more comfortable in an apartment than a hotel room or motel room. I date some white boys who have a lot to lose. They can't afford to be caught coming out of a hotel or motel."

During this opening conversation before the actual interview, Sophie expressed that her days as an escort were coming to an end by showing me a spreadsheet of her potential finances. She had a solid exit strategy in place. I was initially taken back by her candor and openness, but Sophie let me know upfront, "I'm an open book. If you have any questions, ask me. I'll tell you." By showing me her exit strategy, Sophie's goal was to convey that not all transgender women have to spend the rest of their lives working in the sex trade profession. Sophie made clear that "Trans women are more than escorts. But this life just sucks us in. I hope the world doesn't think that we only escort. No, you made us escorts. I had a good job that paid well. Society forced me into this profession. Now, I have a plan to exit this profession."

Before becoming an escort, Sophie had worked in corporate America until she was 26 years old. She lived as a stealth transgender woman longer than she wanted to not "disappoint her family" and fit within a black patriarchal culture. According to Sophie, "I got up in the morning, put on my clothes, and went to work. It was a burdensome routine to a person yearning to express her true gender identity." During this time, co-workers at her place of employment thought that Sophie was a black gay man due to her feminine mannerisms; however, she was really in the transitioning process. Then one day, she showed up to work as a transgender woman. "It was the most uncomfortable, yet liberating day of my entire life," said Sophie. Talking to her during the interview, it was clear Sophie wanted to tell her story to break the societal and cultural silence placed on black transgender women.

My Born Self

"May 16, 2003, I came out. I remember the day like it was yesterday. I woke up and put on a business suit for work. I didn't wear pants. I wore a skirt. I was scared, but then again I wasn't. Looking back on the day, I probably wore a business suit because of fear. I wore [a] skirt [instead of pants] to overcome the fear," said Sophie about the day she came out as a transgender woman. On the day of her transformative rebirth to the world, Sophie proclaimed that it was the most "liberating day of [her] entire life." Her co-workers were in "absolute shock" as she carried along with her day in a usual manner. According to Sophie, only one person inquired about her change in physical appearance and work attire. "This [black] messy bitch tried to mock me and say, 'you look fabulous,' but I didn't care. I knew I looked fabulous."

Throughout the day, Sophie thought her supervising manager and human resources would immediately call her in for a private meeting to discuss workplace protocol. It didn't happen that day. It happened the following day. Sophie described that within weeks the harassment and discrimination became rampant, and eventually she quit. "I quit chile. I couldn't take that shit anymore. I should have fought for my job. The final straw came when my supervisor passed me over for a promotion." In 2003, federal and state protections that ban discrimination based on sexual orientation or gender identity such as the historic passage of the Employment Non-Discrimination Act (ENDA) of 2013 was not enacted to offset such blatant employment discrimination.[2]

The real challenge for Sophie was coming out to her family and friends. Instead of remaining "stealth" and continuing to hide her transgender identity, she also chose to come out to her family the same day she came out at her workplace. Sophie invited her sisters and brothers over to their parent's house. She told them it was a "family emergency." Sophie explained that evening in detail:

> Soooo, like a big dummy, I invited everyone to my parent's house. They already thought that I was gay but had no clue I was transitioning. I went late on purpose. I felt like I could kill all the birds with one stone. Wrong! When my sister opened the door, she was silent. No hug. No nothing. I took about five steps into the house, and my father said, "Boy, get the fuck out of my house dressed like that." I left. I really didn't care. I just needed them to see me as my true self.

She went on to express:

> I'll say this again. It was the most liberating day of my life. Let me tell you why. When I laid my head on the pillow that night, I felt free. I felt free as a bird. The reason I felt free then and do now is that I was born to be a woman. I wasn't molested or raped

as a child. There isn't some crazy reason as to why I wanted to live as a woman. I am a woman. I was born to be a woman. That's exactly what it means to be transgender.

To continue her physical transition, Sophie stated that she had breast augmentation.

The first thing I did was get some titties. You can't be around here looking like a brick with a hard ass chest telling people you're a woman. Everyone ain't tryin' to be passable or even trans for that matter. Some of these bitches are just cross-dressers.

Sophie participated in football and basketball in high school. Through weight training, she had developed a muscular physique. As a consequence of all of those years of participating in athletics, her body needed to be surgically transformed to capture a feminine appearance.

In the beginning, I refused to take hormones, but I needed to break down my muscle mass. I bought estradiol from another trans woman who dated a doctor. I was still kinda burly, so I had to get larger breasts. Then I went and got ass injections. Overall, I think I look good. I don't usually get any complaints from the boys.

When I asked Sophie had she gotten or considered the SRS, she stated at length her reasoning for not getting the bottom surgery:

No, I would never get the bottom surgery because these white boys have all kinds of fetishes. You would really be surprised to know that a lot of these white boys, it's some black ones too, like black trans women because they're infatuated with the size of our penises. The bigger, the better. We're a mystery to them … They desire a sexual unicorn.

I once had a white boy ask me, "Do you have a friend with a big penis like you? I would love for both of you to fuck me." They also like to train munch. As we say in the trans community, "I don't have a dick, I have a pussy stick."

I know this is a lot of information but I just have to say this to dispel all myths about masculinity and being straight or gay. However, there are a lot of white boys and black boys that will set up a date and when we get together, I will hand them a condom and they'll hand it back to me. They'll be like "Here, you put it on you." They want me to do them! They still call themselves straight or heterosexual after that.

Sophie informed me that her physical transition had been harder than her mental transition:

You have to think about this. I've been thinking like a woman all my life. But I've only been living as a trans woman for 13 years. Every trans woman will tell you we're infants in the trans world. That's why you keep hearing me say "boy" and "girl" a lot. In trans years, we're children. I talk in children's language to these men as well. Most of the men who like trans women are children as well to me. They haven't been into trans women for a long period of time. They like when I call them "naughty boy" more than "Daddy." "Daddy" is more of a hetero prostitute term. That's also why I like to school these young trans girls because one day they'll be physically trans longer than they were living as cis. I'm almost there. In 13 years, I'll be 52. Fifty-two baby! That's my golden birthday in the trans world. I physically transitioned at 26 [years old].

She was excited by the thought of celebrating her "golden" birthday. Sophie could then say that she had been living as a transgender woman for the same amount of years as society considered her a cisgender man.

From our discussions, on the initial day and a follow-up interview a couple of months later, Sophie revealed that she has never identified as a black cisgender man. In the first meeting, when repeatedly asked if she has ever identified as a black cisgender man, her answer remained the same, "No." In our second meeting, she finally gave me an answer. Sophie made clear that "Society defined me as a man. I never did that. I lived as a man because I thought I had to. When I realized that I didn't have to, I took steps to change that. That's my best answer."

The need to embrace her true gender identity and deny being medically assigned the sex of male at birth seemed very important. Sophie expressed this before answering the question. "I am who I am." Thus, she wanted to disremember her time and the adversities associated with the social construction of gender that she felt hid her true identity. Sophie insisted "a lot of pressure is placed on us because society will never let us forget we were born with a penis."

I Am a Black Woman, Too

When asked does she believe most members within the black community identify her as a black cisgender woman, Sophie answered, "They better because that's who I am. I am a black woman!" She expounded that the reception among black cisgender people has varied after her transition. Sophie began by describing her interactions with black cisgender men:

> If you're asking a black boy, he'll say among his boys, "That's a dude." Later he'll try to slide me his number. He is curious—bi-curious and trans-curious. The reason he is curious is because I look like a black woman. He is attracted to black women. He sees my features. He likes big titties and a fat ass. Let me ask you this, how can he be

attracted to black women but not be attracted to me when at first sight he doesn't know I'm trans? It's impossible.

I have dated black cis boys before. I still date black cis boys. I just don't accept their money for sex. That changes the dynamics, and they think I'm a piece of property. Hell, I was engaged to a black cis boy and a black trans boy before. I would say it depends on his manhood. Is he comfortable dating me with the chance of someone finding out, especially his boys?

I've had every type of boy from DL's [Downlow], thugs, businessmen, and athletes. You name it, and I've had it. Some of these athletes are admirers [of transgender women]. They just want something different. Most of the athletes whom I've had sex with have been from other professional teams. They come to Houston on a road trip and want some different action. Then they go back home and act like they are straight. I see them on TV, and I just laugh chile.

When asked how black cisgender women react to her identifying as a cisgender woman, Sophie described that their relationship had been a give-and-take of feminine compromise:

There's a crowd of black girls who say, "if you're a woman, I'll accept that and treat you as a woman." They're cool and accepting for the most part. But the majority of black girls see us as a threat. They feel like gay boys and us are a threat to them. I can understand where they're coming from, I really can. It's the other shit that black girls do that drive me crazy like deadnaming us. It's reckless as hell and uncalled for and puts us in danger.

Sophie went on to tell the story about the act of deadnaming, which means to refer to a transgender person by their government name exposing their transgender identity, and it ultimately led to her being chased out of a straight club. She communicated to me the emotional turmoil of the experience:

I was in the club just chillin'. A black cis boy was clocking me. He drummed up a conversation and bought me a couple of drinks. I was having a good ole time, but I wasn't into him at all. I really was in chill mode. When he went to the bathroom, a black cis girl told this nigga that I was trans and my deadname. The next thing I know, him and his friends were standing in front of me ready to beat my ass. I just started swinging and ran out of the club. I hid behind a dumpster until about three in the morning. To this day, I stay out of straight clubs. It's not worth it.

When asked how important it is to pass as a cisgender woman when entertaining clientele, her answer was "It's very important if you want to make a lot of money. Even though the men I deal with know I'm trans; they still want to see me as 100% woman." Sophie stands about 5'8", 165 lbs. Since she doesn't have some of the obvious telltale signs such as large hands, big feet, and a stubbled face, Sophie is able to be passable to "the ordinary non-LGBTQ knowing eye." According to Sophie, "Even when I finish escorting, I will continue to keep myself up and remain passable. I want to be an individual that blends in [to society] and can live an outwardly normal life as a woman."

We Need Protection

At the age of 28 years old, Sophie entered the sex trade profession. After her stint in corporate America, she tried to find employment elsewhere but was met with varying forms of employment discrimination. She applied for multiple jobs and went on several interviews, but there were no call-backs or offers. "I could have lived a stealth life and dressed like a cis man to gain employment, but I felt that it was against everything that I stood for," said Sophie.

When asked why she believes there is an increasing number of black transgender women being murdered within the black community and in the larger American society, Sophie's response was shocking:

> To be honest, some [black] trans girls are provoking these black boys. You already know that these boys don't want anyone to know they are fucking a trans girl. If that is the case, why provoke them? These are young black boys killing these trans girls. You cannot provoke a black cis boy and challenge his manhood. He will kill you. On top of that, some of these young [black] trans girls are HIV-positive, and they don't tell the boys ahead of time.

This response was disconcerting because it gave the impression that she was blaming the victim. In the uncertain translation of risk into deadly harm, her response directly suggests that black transgender women who mislead black cisgender men are culpable and deserve harm for not disclosing their gender identity and/or HIV status. There are cases where victims should bear responsibility; however, deadly harm is not an option.

Sophie told a story about when she provoked a returning client during her early days as an escort after they got into a disagreement about money. "Back in the day, I did service black boys until one of them put a gun to my head," said Sophie in explaining how a client wanted extra services but refused to pay the additional cost. In her description of the violent episode, she detailed:

I always get my money up front. I allowed him to do everything he paid for, nothing more, nothing less. He was a submissive man. I'll spare you the details. He had a lot of fetishes. Toward the end of the act, he had another request. I told him it would be extra. Because he was a regular, I didn't press him and make him pay right then and there.

After we finished, I asked for my money. I said, "Where is my extra $40 dollars?" He refused to pay me. When I got loud and told him, "You got a lil dick anyway, bitch nigga," he pulled a gun out on me. He made me put the barrel of the gun in my mouth as punishment. He scared the shit out of me. I thought I was going to die. He hit me in the back of my head with the butt of the gun. I had to beg him not to pistol-whip me.

Recalling the above violent episode, it was apparent that this incident had an emotional impact on Sophie. As a follow-up question, I asked how she has dealt with the distress of the incident. In her own way of finding a healthy medium to deal with such incidents from recurring, she explained,

That's when I made the decision to only fuck with white boys. All they really want is a good time. Some of them are crazy. But they will only beat you up, not kill you. It's the black cis boys that's fuckin' and killin'. I had to hit the fuck-nigga-kill-switch on them. I couldn't deal with the bullshit. Why is it necessary to kill us?

Pushing back on Sophie's earlier response to the question, "Why do you believe there is an increasing number of black transgender women being murdered," I reframed the question by asking, "Are you saying that black transgender women are to blame for their own deaths?" She clarified by saying:

These young black trans girls be "pussy stuntin". That means they won't tell a cis boy they are trans until they are confronted or forced to, which is fucked up. It only works when girls are passable. They operate under a military code, "Don't Ask, Don't Tell." That code is sometimes getting them murdered. That's what I'm saying.

To provide more context, Sophie described two scenarios where black transgender women who "pussy stunt" are more likely to experience transphobic violence and murders. She attempted to justify her position by elaborating on the violence in the realms of intimate partner violence (IPV) and transgender sex work:

First, most of the trans girls being murdered are young. That's no coincidence. These are young girls who are very passable. If they are dating, most of them date thugs. The first couple of times they are with a black cis boy, they will give him head. A trans girl will do this to make him like her so that when she does spill the tea, he will be comfortable with her being trans. That shit backfires on these young girls. God forbid that someone else spills her tea. The black cis boy will feel disrespected.

If they are escorting, many of them do it in black areas. They live and work in the same areas. Houston is a big city, but the trans world is small. After the black cis boy fucks her, then he doesn't want to see her until he's ready to fuck her again or not at all. If he thinks she will blow his cover or out him, that's it. It's game over, honey. I've seen some shit that if you put it in your book, the cops would be at your front door asking questions.

To close our interview, Sophie was asked does she believe that the black community and the Black Lives Matter (BLM) movement have fought for the humanity of black transgender women. She voiced her frustration by uttering, "Please don't get me started on either one of them. The hashtag #BlackLives-Matter is a fuckin' joke to me." She went on to say:

> None of these people truly care about the lives of trans women of color. They also have Latina girls in the game. It's just that Latino boys have more respect for them than black boys do for us. When I hear "Black Lives Matter," it makes me mad because I know that if I take off this wig my life would matter more than it does with it on. The "Black Lives Matter" movement is a bunch of shit to me. Some black lives matter more than others.

Mia Ryan, 29, Beautician

A black cis man is so dominant and masculine in his own culture. His world is shaken when he encounters and enjoys a trans woman because it goes against everything he has ever been taught about being a man. It mentally confuses him.

—Mia Ryan

Her legal name is now Mia Ryan. This black transgender woman is a promising superstar wrapped in the pain, struggle, and hardship of what it was once like to live her life as the sex she was medically assigned at birth. I first saw Mia on the 2013 Houston-based reality television show, *Houston Beauty*, which aired on the *Oprah Winfrey Network (OWN)*. The show was tailored to chronicle the life of Glenda "Ms. J" Jemison, the owner and director of Franklin Beauty School. However, from the pilot episode of *Houston Beauty*, it was seemingly clear that Mia would be the star of the show. She was a fan favorite. The national audience liked Mia because it was without question that her nonfictional personality would bring a refreshing perspective to a fictional scripted show.

When *Houston Beauty* aired, Mia was only the third transgender woman to have a recurring storyline on a major network TV show. "I wanted to represent transgender women around the world. It's important that people see transgender people in a positive light to dispel all of the preconceived thoughts about us," said Mia. Her appearance on the show was by happenstance. Before enrolling at Franklin Beauty School, she had no prior knowledge that the school would appear on a reality television show. "I'm glad it happened. It has exposed me to the world and opened many doors for me."

Mia's appearance on *Houston Beauty* actually showed her fourth attempt to complete her cosmetology license. According to Mia, "It has been a hard road. It's hard to focus on your dream when you have to also worry about paying bills. The lack of support made my journey longer, but God rewards those who persevere through the struggle." On the show, Mia had to deal with the transgender resistance of Ms. J who identified Mia by using male pronouns and refused to call her Mia but instead referred to her by her birth name, which is Ryan. To compound matters, Ms. J declined to allow Mia to use the women's bathroom. All of these anti-trans actions spoke to Ms. J's religious-driven predisposition that influenced her to disregard the wishes of Mia not to be called Ryan. Despite Ms. J delegitimizing the gender identity of Mia, she still showed Ms. J the utmost respect on the show.

In the process of writing this book, I contacted Mia via Twitter.com to ask for an interview, and she agreed. We met at a Starbucks near the Hobby airport in south Houston. When Mia entered the store, she was dressed to the nines. "Let me order an iced caramel macchiato and banana bread. I need to get right before this interview," she said to the cashier and me simultaneously. It took Mia some time to warm up to the idea of being forthcoming with information about her life despite appearing on national TV. She told me that, "A lot of people try to exploit trans people. You never know what their angle is," before conducting the interview.

From talking to Mia, it was apparent that she had lived a hard life. In a 2013 *Huffington Post* article, she wrote:

> The constant bullying and teasing began during my elementary-school days. I started experiencing both verbal and physical abuse from a majority of my peers. Even worse, I was left with an abusive stepfather who never took the time to understand who I was as a person. Instead, he was determined to recreate my destiny, inflicting a great deal of pain on me and at one point attempting to whip the "gay" out of me.[3]

Mia was thrown out of the house at the age of 13 and left to fend for herself. She soon depended on a life of escorting which she called "survival sex" to have enough money to live independently from her family. She put in plain words to me that her journey to end that lifestyle and start a new one as a beautician has been "a war of morals" but her "primary focus in the last few years." In describing her journey, Mia stated, "I'm now in the process of owning my own beauty salon. I'm on a path that if followed to the end, will leave all my demons behind."

My Born Self

In the beginning of the interview, I asked Mia about a statement she made in a 2014 feature with *Elixher* online magazine. In the piece, she expressed that, "I transitioned to Mia and I totally forgot about Ryan … I'm reaching back out and loving and nurturing and coddling him."[4] In our interview, Mia stated to me that, "I will never forget Ryan. That's why my legal name is Mia Ryan. I want Ryan always to be a part of who I am."

Mia lived her life as a black gay man before eventually deciding to transition to a transgender woman. According to Mia:

I had to do extensive research about the way I was feeling. I know that there is a thick line between being transgender, cross-dressing, and being a drag queen. But, some people are conflicted and confused! I didn't want to be one of those people. Not every individual who claims to be transgender is actually transgender. The name is usually the first attempt to identify with the person to whom you are transitioning to become. Some people change their name and physical appearance but neglect the psychological basis of the transition. Nine times out of ten, it's just a boy who got or is, trapped in their transition.

Mia added to this by stating:

Like I said, there are some individuals identifying as trans because they have begun to change their physical appearance. They get breast implants, ass injections, SRS, and so on. That doesn't make them trans.

To further elaborate on the nature of physically transitioning, Mia explained to me in detail her irresponsible usage of hormones to promote the development of female characteristics. In her description of the chain of events, Mia clearly resented the route she took:

Between the pressure of society and family, I struggled to make decisions based on how I felt rather than how others felt I should live my life. In 2010, I began searching for hormones. There were cruel and dehumanizing experiences that shaped me. One of them was being incarcerated, which made me search even more for ways to transition … I wanted my physical exterior to match the psychological interior. Due to the lack of proper health care, I resorted to dangerous avenues of transitioning. That involved black market silicone and hormones, specifically estrogen.

Back then the process of transitioning through hormone replacement therapy (HRT) had to be first approved by a psychologist after the patient has undergone a psycho-analysis to be deemed a candidate to even receive a referral to a specialist. So, I ordered hormones from the United Kingdom from a site called *In House Pharmacy*.[5] That itself was a major health risk being that the injectables I received had not been approved by the FDA. I self-medicated for a year. I injected one milliliter intramus-cular every seven days, sometimes six and five. It was reckless behavior on my part.

She later explained, "In 2011, I found a transgender specialist here in Hous-ton where I started receiving proper HRT under the supervision of a primary care physician (PCP)." According to Mia, she was "lucky." Mia told me the road to physical transition is not always kind to transgender women.

I tell people don't be insensitive. Don't tease and laugh. A lot of these women are disfigured from getting implants and silicone, and it harms their everyday life. If a cis man is dating a trans woman going through her transition, he should be considerate. She may be hairy in the morning or need to shave. Don't make her feel insecure.

In the 2013 *Huffington Post* article, she expressed that, "Being a transgen-der woman proved even more difficult than being a gay male."[6] I asked if she still felt that way and Mia replied, "Even more so. Living in your truth is the hardest thing in the world to do." In the article, she articulated:

I'd thought to myself, "OK, I have already gone through this whole coming-out phase in my life that has left me without a family unit and lost in society, so becoming a woman should help me blend in more." Boy, was I wrong. Being gay is one thing, but identifying as a trans woman is something entirely different. You wake up feeling a sense of loneliness and longing for someone to tell you that everything is going to be all right. But instead, every day consists of a variety of battles and obstacles that you must continue to fight in hopes that one day you'll win.[7]

Mia reverberated the same sentiments in our interview but when I asked what reactions has she received from members within the black community, she added,

The reaction I've received from most in the black community is pretty much what I expected. Their religious beliefs won't allow them to accept us as people in the eyes of the Lord. Something has to be wrong with us. Nothing is wrong with us. I'm a human being. Something is wrong with you.

I Am a Black Woman, Too

When asked does she believe most members within the black community identify her as a black cisgender woman, Mia answered differently from others interviewed:

> It's impossible for a trans person ever to identify as cisgender. I don't agree when trans women try to identify as "cis" women. "Cis" means non-trans. It's important that trans women identify as who they truly are to continue pushing awareness. Now in terms of sexual orientation and gender identity, there are definitely similarities between cisgender and transgender women who both internally identify as heterosexual women when for the most part both are attracted to heterosexual men. However, anatomically, it's physically impossible in my opinion for anyone who doesn't identify as the gender they were assigned at birth to consider themselves "cisgender."

To clarify her position, I referred back to Mia's earlier response when she stated, "I view myself as a black woman." Inasmuch, I followed this question with asking whether the labels of "cisgender" and "transgender" mattered in the transgender community or are these terms only relevant to academics studying sexualities and gender. She responded, "Yes, both of the terms are important. But to be honest, after your transition, you consider yourself to be a woman. Not a cis or trans woman, but a woman."

I proceeded to ask how black cisgender women react to her identifying as a cisgender woman, Mia explained:

> We all know that most black cis women aren't too enthused by trans women identifying as a combination of their sexual, gender, and cultural identity, and in a different form at that! It intimidates their entire existence. They often find a need to "deadname" and "misgender" us on purpose. They will say, "Hi, Ryan" or "I've been knowing *him* for a long time" in conversations to indirectly demean me [emphasis added].

She went on to explain the dynamics of the relationship between black transgender women and black cisgender women:

> Black cis women can either be a trans woman's best friend or worst enemy. It really all depends on how the two became acquainted. For the most part, both of us share numerous similarities, but when our worlds collide, it's nothing nice. From my experience, black cis women are usually the ones to pick up on some special sense of being when encountering trans in public places and tend to draw attention to us which causes the ridicule and embarrassment. They head nod and do little shit to make people aware that we are trans. When she is angry and scornful, the black cis woman can be very dangerous. I mean very dangerous.

In describing why black cisgender women can become "angry and scornful," Mia pointed out that the root of their venom stems from the competition for a relationship with black cisgender men. She enlightened:

> Since the majority of men attracted to trans women identify as heterosexual, this creates more conflict between the black cisgender and transgender woman. In a sense, we are after the same men. When a black cis woman finds out that a black man is attracted to trans women, she will intentionally try to emasculate him by calling him either "gay," "faggot," or "tranny-chaser." If her goal is to psychologically convert him back per se. She will even use religion to justify her anti-trans agenda.
>
> What these black cis women never really understand is that any type of embarrassment directed toward these men or if he becomes exposed in any sense, that man will feel the need to reclaim his masculinity by any means necessary. This equates to the violence that black trans women are often subjected to that costs us our lives.

When asked do members within the black community treat her different or similar to a black cisgender woman, Mia made it clear in her response that the black community has virtually no respect for the presence of black transgender women. She stated emphatically:

> Most definitely treat us differently! Members of the black community attempt to respond to trans as if we're non-existent. They act like we have no true place in society or in our own community. Don't treat me like shit because you don't understand me. Take the time out to try to understand me. I'm tired of being subjected to mockery and ridicule. Take that shit somewhere else. Black cis people are not perfect. The crazy part is, no matter how attractive or passable a trans woman is the majority of the black demographic will still refer to her as a man!

She ended this part of our interview by discussing that the black community is a "close-minded" community deeply entrenched in the ideologies of the past. "The black community doesn't realize that human life has evolved. Black LGBTQ people didn't just fall out of the sky."

More broadly, Mia's comments reflect the increased frequency of black LGBTQIA people coming out and/or transitioning than in the past. Her description of the black community as "close-minded" speaks to the narrative that black people are egregiously homophobic and anti-trans.

We Need Protection

Mia worked in the sex trade profession for more than a decade before placing that lifestyle behind her. Despite no longer being an escort, she continues to be aware of the transphobic violence and murders affecting black transgender women. When asked why she believes there is an increasing number of black transgender women being murdered within the black community and in the larger American society, Mia provided a lengthy answer:

> There continues to be an increasing number of black trans women murdered in society because violence against us has been ignored. Government agencies and law enforcement do nothing to protect trans people. In the black community, we're sub-human. We're fair game to be murdered. No one will care that we are gone. The system has failed black trans women for many years. When we are discriminated against in the workplace and have no means of employment, we are subjected to sex work, which is really survival sex work. Being excluded from mainstream society places us in a threatened position.

> It's a combination of that and the obsession that the black cis man has with trans women of color. When they deal with us, they feel like their whole identity is comprised subconsciously in their minds because of what the black culture teaches about trans and other LGBTQ people. These black men are convinced that their job is to treat us like shit! It's crazy because society treats them like shit and they turn around and treat us like shit.

> It's so bad. When I would see black cis men as clients, they would walk in [the room] high as a kite and throw the money down and come in with a tone of aggression. Then they would aggressively abuse my body for their own enjoyment. They did it all from just fucking me roughly, choking me, and throwing me around like a rag doll. These men would treat me any kind of way until they reached the point of climax. After it was over, they would get up in disgust because they reacted on natural sexual attraction and gave into the sexual fantasy of being with a trans woman.

> Some would sit there in disbelief. I would think to myself, "believe it, honey." You did it, and you enjoyed it. Some can't even look you in the eyes afterward. If they do, they'll project anger towards you for enticing them. They act like it's my fault they wanted me. There's something about when a man climaxes, his entire aura changes. He becomes a whole other person, which is usually opposite of the side of him that pursued you. This other person can be dangerous when you are dealing with a cis man who has a fragile masculinity.

> A black cis man is so dominant and masculine in his own culture. His world is shaken when he encounters and enjoys a trans woman because it goes against everything he has ever been taught about being a man. It mentally confuses him.

Within the last year, Mia has joined several peer support groups to help transgender women live a healthy and safe lifestyle. She told me during the meetings with other transgender women, they discuss "the pitfalls of the profession and how to stay safe." When asked if she has ever been confronted with transphobic violence and murder, Mia described a near-death experience:

I still have boxes of clothes in Atlanta that I haven't brought home [to Houston] yet. The other day, I ran across a dress. The last time I wore the dress, I almost lost my life. A client that responded to my ad in Atlanta showed up. To make a long story short, he didn't thoroughly read the ad and just looked at the pictures. According to him, he wasn't aware that I was trans. Upon finding out, he started attacking me! If I didn't secretly have a knife, he probably would have killed me. I kept the knife close to me when meeting new clients. I literally had to stab him up to get him off of me.

Mia expounded that before the client attacked her, he called his cousin who was waiting in the car to bring a gun into the hotel room. She gave further details of the incident:

Before stabbing him, he was actually trying to call his cousin who was outside in the car with a "choppa" to come do me in. His blood was all over the place. I kept the dress as a reminder. It symbolizes my past life and how I almost lost it all at the hands of a black man. That was when I stopped seeing black men. They just posed too much of a threat in the escort game.

In the Spring 2016 semester, I invited Mia to speak to one of my classes. In the class discussion, she gave another example as to why she believed black cisgender men murder black transgender women in the form of IPV:

Let's say, for example, a cis man dates you and knows you're trans. There will always be things that awaken him to the realization that you were assigned male at birth like going to the mailbox. He can look at your mail, and it will have your deadname on it. That might trigger something inside of him. Then he may be in a foul mood for the rest of the day, and you don't know why. When he finally tells you, and you dismiss it, it can lead to a very violent situation.

When asked does she believe that the black community and the Black Lives Matter (BLM) movement have fought for the humanity of black transgender women, she responded:

Correct me if I'm wrong, the only inclusiveness of trans with the Black Lives Matter movement that I've seen is a feature on their website. Also, that came after we were being murdered.

I respect that a queer woman help start the organization, but let's be honest, how effective has the BLM been to stop violence in the black community? They only try to protect black men from white police officers.

I haven't seen any political influence or societal impact resulting from the movement to help trans people. I'm sure they have good intentions, but their intentions are not to nationally advocate for black trans women. In the name of BLM, it would be nice to include us.

The frustration of Mia, and the other women interviewed, is rooted in the realism that the BLM's influence is limited to white-black police violence and does not adequately address the dimensions of intra-racial violence within the black community.

Jessica Sugar, 31, Escort

Since coming to the states, I've learned to love my black cis people. I will say though, most of them can kiss my mixed ass. I have a love-hate relationship with them. As much as we have endured as black people, they should be the last people that hate on somebody.
—Jessica Sugar

Jessica Sugar is a 31-year-old black and Filipino transgender woman. Nearly a decade ago, she mentally and physically transitioned and then got SRS. Despite being a dated term in the lexicon of gender and sexuality studies, most scholars of the past would refer to Jessica as a "true transsexual," an individual who by heteronormative standards fully completed the transition. The narrative of Jessica differs from the other case studies not because she has had the SRS but because sex work has been her only means of employment since she was 12 years old. She entered the sex trade profession as a pre-teen massage therapist and eventually became a juvenile sex worker before beginning a life of full-time sex work.

Jessica's father and mother met while he was in the Army and stationed in the Philippines. While dating, her mother became pregnant. Due to the racial difference and age gap in their relationship, Jessica's grandfather didn't grant her mother permission to marry her father and move to the USA. In the early years, Jessica's mother raised her under the strict rules of her grandfather. When she was 11 years old, Jessica's mother sent her to the USA to live with her aunt and uncle for a better quality of life. Her mother was scheduled to follow in the coming months. Unfortunately, her mother took ill during this time and suddenly passed away. Instead of moving back to the Philippines with her grandparents, Jessica was left to live with her aunt and uncle in the states as her legal guardians. According to Jessica, "My grandparents didn't want me [to move] back. They forgot I ever existed."

It wasn't long before Jessica began working in her uncle's massage parlor. She first started as a cashier before being told by her uncle to go in the back and perform massages. "At first, I would just rub the men. I didn't know how to give a massage. The older white men were turned on that a young Filipino girl was giving them a massage," described Jessica. She expounded:

> Later on, the men started to jerk-off in front of me. I guess my uncle gave them permission over time. The more I think about it, the more I think he was a sick fuck. I would service about ten men a night. At that time, it was no sex. I would just rub them, give hand jobs, etc. My shift lasted from 5–9 [p.m.] on most nights. I would only make $25 [a night]. That lasted for about two years.

> One night an older Cuban man, who had come there many times before, gave me $300 and told me not to tell my uncle. I was thinking, "Wow." I worked Thursday to Saturday. That was only $75. I lost my virginity that night and became a full-fledge prostitute all at the same time … At about 15 or 16, I ran away and began working on the streets first and then went to work at another massage parlor.

It was during this period that Jessica Sugar learned how to live on the streets and endure the constant battle of fending for herself. The everyday challenges she faced as a teenager who was also a full-time sex worker trying to avoid pimp-controlled sex work and sexual violence left her with a hard shell to deal with the emotional pain of her family abandonment, abuse, and neglect.

My Born Self

On the day I met Jessica, the city of Houston was under a flash flood warning. A severe thunderstorm had brought heavy rain to the area. We met at the Black Walnut Café, a small eatery place in Rice Village. "Are you William?" she asked in disgust because the rain had wet her new Manolo Blahnik heels. "Yes ma'am," I replied. "Good, I'm [Real Transgender Name]." Jessica's mannerisms were somewhat different from the women I had previously interviewed. This was evident by her attitude, posturing, and how she carried herself.

Before our interview officially began, Jessica told me she was a Triple T (Trannier-than-Thou). This term refers to "someone transgender who has either taken the position or exhibited behavior that indicates their transition was (or is) somehow better than another trans person's … [it] carries with it a lot of attitude and swagger."[8] As Jessica sat down she said to me in a calm voice, "[D]on't be put off by me, I'm a Triple T and I know it. I own that shit."

It was very easy to see how Jessica could adopt a Trannier-than-Thou mentality. It is within this vortex of the transgender world that she has entered. She has the ability to check off all of the so-called Trannier-than-Thou boxes:

She is passable. She has feminine mannerisms. She has gone through voice therapy. She is only attracted to "cis and heterosexual" men. Last, but certainly not least, she has had the SRS.

When asked what does it mean to be transgender, Jessica explained in her own words that, "Being transgender means to love the person whom you are born as. I was born as a woman. I had a penis, but I was born as a woman. I don't buy into sex or gender roles." Since Jessica did not "buy into sex or gender roles," I followed by asking why did she have the SRS? She answered:

> I got the SRS because I wanted to be a complete woman. I have a vagina now but having a vagina doesn't make you a complete woman, it's all of the other things from appearance to the way you carry yourself. Be honest. When you look at me, you don't see trans. You see a beautiful black woman. Even though I'm mixed, black is clearly the dominant gene. My father is a dark-skinned black man.

Our time at the Black Walnut Café was not without a scene. "I wanted the gluten-friendly pancake stacks, and you brought me buttermilk pancake stacks," she said to the help staff after refusing to pick up her food from the counter. I asked Jessica about her refusal to pick up the food from the counter. With a side-eye, she said:

> Chile, I have a DD cup and an ass full of silicone. I don't just prance around in public places and bring a lot of attention to myself. I once had a man follow me to the bathroom and was waiting outside of the stall when I came out with his dick in his hand.

Jessica's mannerisms were clearly different from the other black transgender women interviewed. As a result, I had to get to the bottom of this self-proclaimed, Trannier-than-Thou mentality. I asked if we could go back to our conversation about being Trannier-than-Thou and requested more answers to understand why she has embraced this persona:

> There are two reasons, really. The first part of it is that my life has been hard. I was turned out at a very young age by my uncle. He took my fuckin' childhood away from me. He had me doing shit that a 12-year-old should never do. I lost count of the number of men I was with and dicks I jerked under his supervision. [paused to collect her thoughts] It made me numb to the idea of being called a little boy, young man or man. Maybe my uncle saw a feminine side of me. Maybe he saw me as a ladyboy, but it wasn't his choice to make. When I got the top and bottom surgeries, in my mind, it validated a life that I was already living.

The second part of her reason for embracing the Trannier-than-Thou mentality spoke to the contentious relationship between transgender women who are deemed "passable" versus those who prefer just "being recognized." As noted in Chapter 2, some transgender women reject the wanting to be considered "very passable." Jessica clarified:

I'm Triple T because I take on the natural elements of womanhood.

When so many other trans women are referring to me as a "sellout" because I've taken personal steps to be the woman I believe I should be, being Triple T is a shield against these hatin' ass trans bitches. We ain't all one big happy family. I hope you didn't think that. There's a lot of competition among us. A lot of hatin' out here.

Jessica indicated that her transgender identity has evolved over time and stating publicly that she is Triple T is one of those changes. "People hate on me, but they respect me because I demand respect. I'm not a tramp or streetwalker. I'm a sophisticated woman. I'm a true trans."

When asked what reactions have she received from family and friends, Jessica was very forthcoming with the fact that she has not maintained a relationship with her family in the Philippines. She pointed out:

I don't have a relationship with any of my family in the Philippines. My mother died. My grandmother has now died. My grandfather didn't want me to return after my mother died. My aunt and uncle are dead to me. I'm most mad at my aunt. She knew what was going on and let it happen. I don't have any family at all.

I followed that question up to inquire if she had found her father and established a relationship with him:

I have contacted my father a couple of times. I saw him once, and that was before I had my surgeries. Let me think, that was more than ten years ago. We have a stealth relationship. When we met that one time, I dressed up as a guy. He lives in Washington, D. C. He has an ex-wife and three other kids that don't know about me ... He's never even been to Houston. My father thinks I work at an insurance company. It's all good.

She went on to say, "I should come clean with my father about my true identity. However, since he doesn't care enough about me to keep in contact, I don't care enough about him to tell him about the woman his little boy has become. It's my personal choice."

Except for her late mother, Jessica's immediate family failed her. Her earliest memories of them involved "alienation," and "sex," which is a deadly combination to a young person looking for acceptance. When asked why did she think her uncle placed her in a threatening position in the massage parlor,

Jessica stated while tearing up, "I've racked my brain trying to figure that out for years. I've only come to one conclusion. It was because I'm part black. He didn't like black people. He always called black people 'niggers' even though he knew I was black as well. So I'm guessing he didn't fully like or love me. Either way, he is dead to me."

I Am a Black Woman, Too

At the ripe age of 21 years old, Jessica "was a complete woman," as she described the confirmation of her physical transition with SRS.

> I know people will think that getting turned out led to my decision to transition to trans and get the surgery but it wasn't at all. I could have lived as a gay man. All of that just awakened something inside of me. I was born a girl. I'm going to die a woman.

When asked does she believe most members within the black community identify her as a black cisgender woman, Jessica unequivocally responded, "Yes, they do. I look better than a lot of these women out there. You line up 100 women right now I bet black cis men will choose me every time. I'm that confident!" She went on to explain that most black cisgender men treat her different than other black cisgender women because "[T]hey really can't tell I used to be a man. I'm 5'4", 125 lbs., with a DD cup, and a fat ass. Not like some other trans women, I have softer features. I started hormones at about 18."

When asked was the fact that she perceived herself as "very passable" the main reason why black cisgender men found her attractive, Jessica replied:

> No, that's not the main reason. Even before I had the bottom surgery, I had a small she-meat [i.e., penis]. That made men more likely to see me as a woman or a person that they wanted to be with for a longer time and maybe start a relationship. The men that like trans women with big dicks are usually just tranny chasers. They don't want a relationship with them. They are just side pieces for them.

She went on to say:

> I settled with being the side bitch before. I won't do that again. I'll never do that again. I need a cis man to accept me for who I am, a beautiful black woman. The game needs to be right. I don't want an old ass, ready to die cis man. The older ones don't care. They'll walk around with you in public. They don't care what people think. They will flaunt us to the world. But I'm tired of the old cis men. I need a young, vibrant cis man with a strong identity who won't crack under the pressure of being with a trans woman. I don't want to hide the fact that I used to have male body parts.

When asked how black cisgender women react to her identifying as a cis-gender woman, Jessica initially hesitated on answering the question. "It's like I told you before, we ain't all one big happy family. I get hate from trans women and from cis women," said Jessica. She explained in detail how transgender women and cisgender women had treated her over the years:

Trans women, as you can probably guess, have a problem with me. It's that Triple T thing again. I once had a trans woman who I thought was a friend set me up. She told two guys where I lived, and they all came to my apartment. She knocked on the door, and when I opened the door, the two guys attacked me. This is going to sound sick, but they all took turns raping me even the trans bitch … It was a fucked up situation. I thought trans women were supposed to stick together.

In her depiction of black cisgender women, Jessica told another disturb-ing story about a woman who "spilled [her] tea" to a bunch of black cisgender men who thought she was a cisgender woman. "Well, basically they cornered me and beat my ass," said Jessica. In describing the scenario, she pointed out that one of the men had asked for her number a couple of months before the attack. Because she hadn't given him her number, he felt as though Jessica was "playing hard to get … and trying to deceive him. I wasn't trying to deceive him. I knew his ass was crazy." According to Jessica:

The bottom line was that his feelings were hurt. When the girl spilled my tea and told him I was trans in front of his boys, he felt dumb as hell. They basically jumped me. The funny thing is, they thought I still had a penis. They didn't know I had bottom surgery. They ripped off my clothes to try to embarrass me. Well, I was embarrassed. When they saw I didn't have a penis, one of them said, "that's not a boy." I took off running as fast as I could into a convenience store. Lord, I didn't want them to rape me. About six months later, I saw one of them, and he apologized and asked for my phone number. The gall of some of these black motherfuckers.

His apology, unsurprisingly, fell upon unreceptive ears as Jessica was fright-ened to return to that area of the city again. "These cis men have long memo-ries. You have to be careful when fuckin' with them. I told him I accepted his apology so he could move on."

It was important to ask Jessica about her SRS. When asked how she paid for the SRS, Jessica responded:

One of them old ass ready to die, white cis men, I was talking about earlier. No, let me be real. He was a sweet man. He was my daddy. Not my real daddy, you know what I mean. He took really good care of me.

The man who Jessica described served as an influential surrogate during her physical transition. She explained how the nature of their relationship changed over time:

> We dated for about two years. The crazy part is, he still allowed me to work. However, after I got cut [i.e., SRS], that was when he became jealous. He didn't want me to work anymore. In the strangest way, he was more comfortable with men having anal sex with me [before SRS] than vaginal sex [after SRS]. That made him very jealous and led to some heated arguments.

During our interview, Jessica showed her gratitude for the role he played in her life. "He recently died from a heart attack. I went to the funeral. No one knew who I was, but I got a chance to meet his ex-wife and children. It gave me a glimpse into his life before we met," she said. "I owe him a lot. He helped to validate me as a complete woman."

We Need Protection

Throughout the interview, Jessica expressed affection for her black roots. There was an affirmation toward the black side of her mixed lineage that led me to ask her how she felt the black community treated black transgender women:

> Since coming to the states, I've learned to love my black cis people. I will say though, most of them can kiss my mixed ass. I have a love-hate relationship with them. As much as we have endured as black people, they should be the last people that hate on somebody.

When asked why she believes there is an increasing number of black transgender women being murdered within the black community and in the larger American society, Jessica pointed to three reasons: (1) "Unpassable," (2) "Not selective enough," and (3) "Too brash."

> God forgive me when I say this, but some of these bitches are unpassable. I mean, they aren't even trying. There are a bunch of transzillas on Backpage.com. When you look at their profiles, it's like "ugh." Those are the trans that have to settle for making money any way that they can. Those are also the trans whom men have to get really high to fuck to make themselves believe they are fucking a woman. When that high wears off, they question what the fuck they've just done. Then they play stupid and ask the trans girl questions like, "What did we do? Did we have sex?" Their manhood is in jeopardy now. So they act out.

In explaining how she now sets up dates with her clients to be more selective, Jessica stated:

> No offense to you or nothing but I don't set up dates with black cis men. I used to date black cis men, but I had to stop that shit. On my profile, I make sure to say two things: First, I'm "100%" woman. Second, "No black men." When I did set up dates with black cis men before the surgery, they were too aggressive and rough. They would smack me around during sex. It was just too much to handle. Right after the surgery, I serviced one client who I had been with before, and he claimed that I tricked him because I now had a vagina. And because I tricked him, he said he deserved to go in me raw. I said, "hell no." He beat me and stole all my money.

> I rarely work the streets anymore. I do a lot of referrals. I give these white cis men my Snapchat. We snap a couple of times and set up an appointment. This way I avoid all of the drama and live to talk about it. I can't live in fear.

According to Jessica, the last reason for the increased number of black transgender women being murdered is that some of the women are "too brash." She explained:

> Some of these bitches need to keep their mouths closed. They're too brash. They want to be women, but in confrontations with men, they act like men. It becomes a dick-swinging contest. Well honey, you've been taking hormones. You aren't as strong as a man to beat his ass. If you do beat his ass, threaten to expose him, or anything remotely close, he'll find you and murder you. I'm not saying these women deserve to be murdered, but I'm saying that if you chose this lifestyle, there are consequences. So you have to know that.

> Each time I was assaulted or feared for my life was in the presence of a black cis man. White men love me, honey. Hispanic men love me. Asian men adore me. But see, these black cis men are a trip. After I help them fulfill one of their sexual fantasies, it makes them question their manhood. Even though I have a vagina now, just the thought that I had a penis before intimidates them.

I asked Jessica how and why does the conversation of exposing the man's sexual preference come up in the topic of conversation between black cisgender men and black transgender women. For clarity, I wanted to know whether being "too brash" extended to "outing" a man who tried to demean them in any way:

> These men are a trip. Especially y'all black cis men. Y'all say that you're heterosexual when you sleep with us because you're attracted to our appearance of being female. Before I had a vagina, men would say, "I'm not gay because you look like a female. If I had sex with a man who looks like a man, then I'd be gay." Chile, please! In

both cases, he would be having anal sex … When these trans women sense this type of insecurity or know this, they use it to their advantage to ask for more money or threaten to spill his tea. It may set that man off in the worse way.

For nostalgia sake, and to be fair to the other women interviewed who have not had the SRS, I asked Jessica why would she still be living life as a transgender sex worker after the surgery which in her words made her a "complete woman" and continue to expose herself to potential risks and danger. She responded:

The truth is, it's all I've ever known how to do. Some days I ask myself was the whole transition worth it if I'm still selling my body. Why am I still doing this? I mean, the money is good but is it worth it you ask? Last week I was with a white guy who was into erotic asphyxiation but he wanted to choke me. He got off on choking me while he was fucking me. This motherfucker almost choked me to death. Luckily he came before he choked the life out of me. These white guys can be dangerous, too. But to answer your question, it's all I know.

When asked does she believe that the black community and the Black Lives Matter (BLM) movement have fought for the humanity of black transgender women, Jessica defended the black community and the BLM movement; however, she indicated that "more work needs to be done." She explained in her response:

I'm sure the Black Lives Matter movement has good intentions. We've seen that with all the murders of black men. But when it comes to us, more work needs to be done. March for us. Protest for us. When Tyra Underwood was murdered, what did they do? Absolutely nothing. Didn't the boy who murdered her yell, "I'll be back on the streets" in the courtroom? That should have been enough right there for them to get involved. If a white man like [George] Zimmerman would have yelled that in court, them Black Lives people would be all over that.

Jessica ended our interview by recommending that the BLM movement should take a "long and hard look at these trans panic defenses" and address the "unfair justice" for black transgender women.

Conclusion

To better understand the complexities of the lived experiences of black transgender women, this chapter has provided more insight into the extensive systemic, institutional, and interpersonal circumstances that affect black transgender to evaluate how they can survive in the embattlement of every-day life. The themes presented were: (1) "My Born Self," (2) "I Am a Black Woman, Too," and (3) "We Need Protection." Each of these themes was consistent with the literature from the preceding chapters.

Derived from the narratives within the themes, and input from the other black transgender women interviewed, we can again extract the most consistent discoveries throughout the chapters: (1) The reinforcement that societal, cultural, and gender norms are the mitigating circumstances that hinder black transgender women from acceptance and inclusion after their transition, (2) Patriarchal violence within the black community toward black cisgender women has extended to black transgender women, and (3) Toxic masculinity among black cisgender men who consider themselves heterosexual poses a grave threat to black transgender women. The other substantive conclusions were: (4) Toxic femininity among black cisgender women, as well, has been detrimental to black transgender women, and (5) Black transgender women do not believe that the black community and the BLM movement have made significant strides to assist in their human survival and well-being.

Notwithstanding the hate-based violence that targets transgender people, the number of black transgender women murdered in recent years reveals an ugly truth about the toxic masculinity that condones such violence against these women. According to Sophie Rush, "These are more than hate crimes. Without pathologizing them, these [black cisgender] men enjoy a piece of us that brings some sort of gratification. They hate themselves because they like the pleasure we give them. I had a black cis boy tell me once, 'I love you, but if you tell anybody [about us], I'll kill you.' That messed me up."

From Chapters 1 through 4, the most substantive recommendation from the black transgender women interviewed to black cisgender men who consider themselves to be heterosexual (or straight), despite engaging in domestic relationships with transgender women or soliciting sexual services from transgender sex worker, has been to make more of a conscious and responsible effort to align with their stated sexual orientation. If these black cisgender men truly align with heterosexuality, it is in the best interest of the black community and larger LGBTQIA community for them not to venture into same-sex relationships or transgender relationships, and then hide behind a patriarchal shield that empowers them to exercise a toxic form of masculinity absent of reciprocal humanity.

Further unpacking from the narratives can be pivoted into many directions that either intentionally or unintentionally pathologizes black cisgender men. First, as pointed out in Chapter 3 and this chapter, black transgender women who work in the sex trade profession indicate that the black cisgender men whom they service are more violent than white cisgender men. From such a limited sample, can we validate through their experiences that black cisgender men are more toxic, aggressive, hypersexual, and violent? Second, is it possible to simplify this argument as one where geographical proximity is the main culprit that promotes such intra-racial violence? Third, what is the latitude given to black cisgender men who have been raised under the reli- gious-driven phobias constructed by the social institution of the black church and are afraid to openly explore their true sexual preference in black public spaces? Fourth and last, but certainly not least, do we take into account the fragile masculinity of black cisgender men created from adverse structural and cultural forces? By no means are black cisgender men absolved in any shape, form, or fashion by identifying these internal and external factors germane to the black community and culture. Without a shadow of the doubt, the onus lies solely on them to respect all human life despite their circumstances.

Notes

1. John Nova Lomax in a 2006 *Houston Press* article titled, "The Sole of Houston" described Westheimer Road as "Nowhere is the 'anything goes' image that adheres to Houston more blatantly displayed than along the stretch of Westheimer Road." Available at: http://www.houstonpress.com/news/the-sole-of-houston-6545147.

2. For more information on S. 815: Employment Non-Discrimination Act of 2013, see a full description of the legislation. Available at: https://www.congress.gov/bill/113th-congress/senate-bill/815

3. See Hogues, M. 2013. "Finding my place as a transgender woman." *HuffingtonPost.com*. Available at: http://www.huffingtonpost.com/mia-hogues/finding-my-place-as-a-transgen-der-woman_b_4185114.html? (November 1).

4. Ailith, L. J. 2014. "Houston beauty breakout star Mia Ryan is walking in her truth." *ELIX-HER.com*. Available at: http://elixher.com/houston-beauty-breakout-star-mia-ryan-is-walking-in-her-truth (January 22).

5. The following description of *In House Pharmacy* is found on their webpage. It reads, "InhousePharmacy.vu is one of the worlds original and longest standing online pharmacies established in 1996. We only supply non-restricted medicines that we source from FDA approved manufacturers." For more information: https://www.inhousepharmacy.vu

6. Hogues, Finding my place as a transgender woman.

7. Ibid.

8. See Ennis, D. 2016. "10 words transgender people want you to know (but not say)." *Advo-cate.com*. Available at: http://www.advocate.com/transgender/2016/1/19/10-words-trans-gender-people-want-you-know-not-say (February 4).

References

Meyer, D. 2008. Interpreting and experiencing anti-queer violence: Race, class and gender differences among LGBT hate crime victims. *Race, Gender & Class* 15(3–4): 262–282.

Meyer, D. 2010. Evaluating the severity of hate-motivated violence: Intersectional differences among LGBT hate crime victims. *Sociology* 44(5): 980–995.

· 5 ·

BLACK TRANS LIBERATION

I have often not felt safe in America as a trans woman of color. Often I have not been safe. That trauma is real. The reality of systemic oppression is ever present in the lives of trans people, women, people of color.
—Laverne Cox, November 9, 2016 via Twitter[1]

This book has examined societal and cultural issues and concerns related to the humanity of black transgender women. The previous chapters have provided significant findings that should be of great use in the future as more scholars across the different academic disciplines examine the lived experiences of this understudied group. The overarching questions guiding this book have been: *What are the implications for black transgender women medically assigned the sex of male at birth but have chosen to exercise their right to identify as a transgender and/ or gender non-conforming person within the black community, which has historically shown a propensity to promote a toxic masculinity within the context of a black patriarchal culture and suppress any form of femininity in black men? How, then, do black transgender women live as black women within a black patriarchal culture that facilitates toxic masculinity? Can the black community and Black Lives Matter movement progress in a unified direction to protect the humanity of black transgender women?*

In an attempt to answer these questions, this book focused on the toxic masculinity that threatens the humanity of black transgender women. The guiding framework centered on giving them a voice to address the increase of transphobic discrimination, violence, and murders. In this regard, the book investigated what it means to be a black transgender woman within the black community and in the larger American society, what is the societal and cultural impact of the black male-to-black female (MtF) transition on black masculinity and black femininity, and when will we, as a gendered American culture, address the deadly effects of toxic masculinity within the black community that leads to violence against black transgender women.

This book began with the presumption that black people of all ages, creeds, color variations, sexes, national origins, religions, sexual orientations, gender identities, disabilities, marital statuses, and socioeconomic statuses are an interdependent group. As such, all black voices in the group must be heard, and their lives must matter to achieve collective group action to further the interests of blacks in American society. Moving throughout the chapters, I have attempted to identify whether there is a symbiotic relationship between the mission of the black community and the Black Lives Matter (BLM) movement as a whole to fight to secure justice for black transgender women in the same manner as unarmed black men shot and killed at disproportionately rates by white law enforcement officers, violence against black women, and intra-racial violence among black people. Each has sparked protests and outrage around the country. During the call to secure justice for these black men and black women, left from the complete narrative has been the focused attention to the forms of structural and cultural violence against black LGBTQIA people, specifically the number of black transgender women murdered during the same time period.

Broadly, the evidence reported in this book confirms that a patriarchal system of male domination breeds a form of toxic masculinity that plays a deadly role in the widespread rate of transphobic violence and murders. To begin, the black church as a social institution has contributed to this oppressive dynamic by maintaining a set gender hierarchy within the black culture leading to a multigenerational effect. Borrowing from Cohen (1999), the issue of black transgender deaths is cross-cutting and partly the reason for it not gaining more awareness from the black church, which would prioritize the need to address the transphobic violence and murders toward them. Instead, it is not perceived as an issue that the black church as a whole should outwardly address because that would possibly signal their approval of the gender identity of black transgender women. As a result, secondary marginalization provoked by the black church has the potential to increase the rate of black transgender women who are murdered within the black community.

This framework as well is enforced in the black household through normative ideas about gender that has created an artificial construction of black masculinity suppressing black femininity. Normative beliefs about what it means to be a man or a woman have been detrimental to the formation of attitudes about gender, sexuality, and gender identity. The 2016 movie, *Moonlight*, provides an admirable example of the dismantling of black masculinity within the black community. The film is divided into three parts, titled "Little," "Chiron," and "Black." Each part provides insight into the gender expression of black males.[2] In an American society and black community and culture with rapidly changing gender identities, roles, appearances, and characteristics, the artificial construction of black masculinity has had an adverse effect on black male gender expression.

In order to more fully understand the hate-based violence, intimate partner violence (IPV), and violence against transgender sex workers, an intersectional approach explained how these situational and cultural contexts lead to violence against black transgender women. The gender-based violence against these women from black cisgender men must continue to be analyzed and addressed from an intersectional approach to gain more awareness of the systemic, institutional, and interpersonal practices that perpetuate forms of structural and cultural violence.

There is a powerful and essential connection between the macro-level and micro-level constructs that lends itself to the multiple moving parts to address the yearly increase in the deaths of black transgender women. The culmination of these constructs has birthed a gendered American culture that believes only one gender, one sexual orientation, and one gender identity exists, one dominating all others. As I have argued, within the black patriarchal culture, toxic masculinity is the aggressive and violent filter to eliminate any conflation among gender, sexual orientation, and gender identity. Even more detrimental, this form of masculinity assists to ensure that this rigid gender binary is maintained at all costs. The multiple intersections of these constructs work at every turn to prevent the normalization of black transgender women.

The toxic masculinity exhibited by some black cisgender men against black transgender women does not exist in a vacuum. This is a complex problem as described in the preceding chapters. This patriarchal violence stems from taught societal and cultural oppression through a vessel of historical white supremacy that teaches black cisgender men to be so-called "real men" free of vulnerability and expressions that counter hegemonic masculinity. Cohen (2014) identifies that one of the most difficult and challenging parts about properly describing such violence within the black community is to avoid pathologizing the behaviors that exist in this communal makeup. And more importantly, reject the assumed pathological identities of black cisgender men and develop a greater understanding of the authoritative nature and structure of white supremacy that maintains a structural advantage over them in nearly every aspect of their human life.

The growing and increasingly important belief derived from the interviews with black transgender women is that the attention toward their deaths is neglected due to black cisgender men being the wrongdoers. According to their premise, the black community as a whole has turned a blind eye to protect the heteropatriarchy embedded within the community. Moreover, it situates by default the black community as a singular entity in which the cultural relationship between the people and the community as a whole operates as a homogenized community.

Even more problematic to this premise, the black community as a whole is presented as more patriarchal, heteronormative, homophobic, and transphobic than other communities. As a result, it strongly implies that the black community is entirely responsible for the cultural climate that facilitates the transphobic violence and murders toward black transgender women rather than understanding how systems of oppression often structure the lives of black transgender women. It is important to stress that many of the black transgender women in this book while narrating their lived experiences, struggled with the notion of pathologizing the entire black community by explaining the actions and behaviors of some black cisgender men. Nonetheless, they told their truths when explaining the transphobic violence and murders against them. For these women, this is not a racial secret, but a cultural truth told from their perspectives.

This book acknowledges and understands the importance of telling this cultural truth without pathologizing the entire black community. The point is that, in a context in which black cisgender men are murdering black transgender women, this reality must be explained according to Cohen (2014, p. 484) without being bound to "a tradition of pathologizing the behaviors of the African-American poor and working class." In a review of the pathologizing of black deviance comparing past and present black research from the likes of Elijah Anderson and William J. Wilson, Cohen indicates that through the rigorous examination of the lived experiences within the black community, a mechanism of pathology is often developed. However, it is incumbent upon the researcher to reject the assumed pathological identities of those who commit such deviance and violence with no account for the normative structures in place that often affect the most vulnerable within the black community. Cohen argues, "At the root of such judgments sits an unexamined acceptance of normative standards of association, behavior" (p. 484).

The black cisgender men who commit such violence are following a fixed masculine script and do not believe that they are at cultural liberty to adhere to the sliding scale of masculinity. As a result, for some of them, patriarchal and heteronormative frames have worked to suppress their true sexual orientation. When these black cisgender men do act on their sexual desires behind closed doors, it often leads them to question their masculinity and use toxic violence to psychologically reverse the mental component of the act and to regain masculine control of the situation.

Acknowledging that a patriarchal social structure is working to maintain the multiple intersections that victimize black transgender women within the black community and in the larger American society leads to the following questions: How can the black community and the BLM movement progress in a unified direction to protect the humanity of black transgender women? What is the fit for black transgender women within a mainstream black community where black elites have a rank and file approach for addressing societal and cultural issues and concerns? According to the women interviewed, it is firmly believed that there is a gap between the intentions of the social activism of members within the black community and BLM movement when it comes to addressing transgender rights and protections. Despite the BLM movement encompassing LGBTQIA people in prominent and central leadership roles, their influence has yet to reach the masses of black people, and it appears that the movement is on the verge of losing total momentum in the Trump presidential era.[3] To this end, there needs to be a push of solidarity for members in general within the black community to take on a larger role of responsibility, along with politicians and community leaders, for the equal rights and protections of black transgender women to preserve their humanity.

National Day of Remembrance

November 20th is Transgender Day of Remembrance (TDoR). Gwendolyn Ann Smith, a transgender woman, founded the day in 1999 to honor the death of another transgender woman, Rita Hester. Every year in the USA and abroad this day represents an opportunity for all individuals to come together and pay their respects to transgender and gender non-conforming people who have lost their lives in the past year. According to the U.S. Department of State in recognizing the magnitude of such a day:

> [W]e stand in solidarity with the incredible resilience and leadership of the transgender community in responding to stigma and marginalization. Transgender persons deepen our diversity, broaden our communities, and strengthen the values we cherish. When all persons reach their full human potential, free from fear, intimidation, and violence, nations become more just, secure and prosperous.[4]

On August 26, 2015 another historical day was marked in American history. This day titled, Black Trans Liberation Tuesday,[5] was a call to action to raise public awareness and promote activism to combat the deaths of black transgender women.[6] In response to the criticism that the BLM movement had not been responsive to their deaths, on this inaugural day members of the movement and other black groups organized a National Day of Action.[7] BLM organizing coordinator, Elle Hearns of Washington, D. C., was instrumental in organizing this event that created a platform for cisgender and transgender people to come together in support of black transgender women.

One of the bright moments of the events was when black cisgender men and women were invited to the stage to denounce violence against these women. Timothy DuWhite, who is an LGBTQIA activist, expressed empathetically to the audience in a state of contrition, "We are the murderers" when discussing the violence against black transgender women and the importance of accountability for black cisgender men.[8] Upon reflecting on the inaugural event, DuWhite wrote an online blog post titled, "Why black men must show up for trans-women of color." He articulated in the post:

> This day was created as a space where communities all across the nation could collectively mourn and speak out against the extreme violence black trans-women and gender non-conforming femmes face on a daily basis.

> Black liberation can not be compartmentalized. As long as black trans-women remain oppressed and pushed to the margins we all remain oppressed and pushed to the margins.

> The truth of the matter is a lot of these murders are at the hands of cis-black men (majority are presumed lovers). So often we as black folk are afraid to acknowledge the violence within our own community out of fear it will just be used against us and deferred to a racist "black on black crime" trope. However, it is important for us to acknowledge that yes, a lot of these murders of trans women of color are at the hands of cis black men. Yet, this in no way negates the terror of the violence enacted against the black community as a whole by racist, white supremacist structures.[9]

Imani Brown, a member of the Black Youth Project 100, spoke on behalf of black cisgender women. She conveyed that, "We [black cisgender women] know what it's like to be erased. Yet, we are also guilty of enacting that violence."[10]

Both the Transgender Day of Remembrance and Black Trans Liberation Tuesday are important days in the annals of American history for all people to remember transgender and gender non-conformity people who have lost their lives. Despite the mourning around the day, these vigils give transgender people faith, hope, and courage to keep working to eradicate the barriers of resistance and highlight the scope of transgender issues and concerns to build levels of solidarity.[11] When explaining the importance of the continuation of Black Trans Liberation Tuesday, Elle Hearns articulated during the 2016 second anniversary that in the previous year, "Black trans folks had been experiencing erasure from the movement and a lack of support from cis people that we'd been in solidarity with who hadn't reciprocated that support," however with the help of one of the co-founders, Patrisse Cullors, the transphobic violence and murders related to black transgender women would move to be more of a priority for the movement.[12]

Where Do We Go from Here?

The larger LGBTQIA community, in general, has witnessed significant social and political gains within the last decade. From the Matthew Shepard and James Byrd, Jr., Hate Crimes Prevention Act to the legalization of same-sex marriages to the increasing visibility and marginal acceptance of transgender people, it is incontestable that strides were made in the USA. A 2016 poll by the Public Religion Research Institute (PRRI) reported that 72% of Americans were in favor of passing additional laws to protect LGBTQIA people from practices of discrimination.[13] And when controlling for race, approximately two-thirds (65%) of black Americans were in favor of such protections.[14] Such results suggest that the myth of overwhelming black homophobia appears to be waning within the black community.

According to MSNBC journalist, Adam Talbot, despite such strides made for the LGBTQIA community, "The truth is that the equality LGBT people have won in this country is incomplete, new, brittle, and it faces a blistering counterattack on all fronts."[15] The brittleness of the status of LGBTQIA people, in my opinion, is most likely to continue to affect black LGBTQIA people. When we factor the role that socially constructed identities present, it centers more toward the victimization of black transgender women than other variations of black LGBTQIA people and their lives because the intersections of race, gender identity, and socioeconomic status make them one of the most vulnerable in the conversation to guarantee equal rights and protections.

To combat the violence against black transgender women, the challenges in which they face must be met with solution-based recommendations to the systemic, institutional, and interpersonal circumstances that confront them. According to Mia Ryan:

> All black trans women want is inclusion with no strings attached. Let us live with our identity and not the ones created to hurt us. We don't want tolerance, we want acceptance. We want the government to fight on our behalf. We want the people to fight on our behalf. It's time for us to be treated equally.

Her position builds on the societal and cultural reception that black transgender women wish to receive from within the black community and in the larger American society.

Solution-Based Recommendations

Here I identify three solution-based recommendations to the systemic, institutional, and interpersonal circumstances that confront black transgender women. The recommendations are not exhaustive, but they do mirror the most substantive issues and concerns discussed in this book.

The first recommendation is to continue the fight for the equal rights and protections of the LGBTQIA community. During his eight years in presidential office, Barack H. Obama and his Administration were strong advocates of the LGBTQIA community.[16] Richard Socarides, who was President Clinton's top adviser on LGBTQIA issues and concerns, in his evaluation of Obama's legacy has argued that, "[H]is record on gay rights will be one of his most important and lasting accomplishments."[17] As noted in Chapter 3, in 2009 he signed "The Matthew Shepard and James Byrd, Jr., Hate Crimes Prevention Act." In June of the same year, he ordered a directive on same-sex domestic partner benefits.[18] In March 2010 under the Affordable Health Care Act, he added a clause that insurance companies could not discriminate on the basis of sexual orientation and gender identity.[19] During December of 2010, he signed a bi-partisan piece of legislation repealing the 1993 "Don't Ask, Don't Tell" (DADT) law allowing LGBTQIA people to serve in the military openly.[20]

In February 2011, Obama and the former Attorney General, Eric H. Holder Jr., decided it was time to end the Defense of Marriage Act (DOMA), which defined marriage as only between a man and woman. Both of the men cited that the 1996 law, which banned the federal recognition of same-sex marriages was unconstitutional. In a statement justifying their decision, Holder indicated:

> After careful consideration, including a review of my recommendation, the President has concluded that given a number of factors, including a documented history of discrimination, classifications based on sexual orientation should be subject to a more heightened standard of scrutiny.[21]

In July 2014, he signed an executive order prohibiting federal contractors from discriminating on the basis of sexual orientation or gender identity.[22] The momentum from the Obama Administration led to the landmark 2015 U.S. Supreme Court decision allowing same-sex marriage. After the U.S. Supreme Court ruling, Obama stated in support of the court's decision:

> Our nation was founded on a bedrock principle that we are all created equal. The project of each generation is to bridge the meaning of those founding words with the realities of changing times—a never-ending quest to ensure those words ring true for every single American.

> It's a victory for gay and lesbian couples who have fought so long for their basic civil rights. It's a victory for their children, whose families will now be recognized as equal to any other. It's a victory for the allies and friends and supporters who spent years, even decades, working and praying for change to come.

> Folks who were willing to endure bullying and taunts, and stayed strong, and came to believe in themselves and who they were, and slowly made an entire country realize that love is love.[23]

To commemorate the court's decision, he had the White House illuminated in rainbow colors. In a press conference discussing the rainbow illumination of the White House, Obama commented that, "[T]o see people gathered in the evening on a beautiful summer night and to feel whole and to feel accepted and to feel they had a right to love, that was pretty cool. That was a good thing."[24]

In May 2016, the Obama Administration came under a firestorm of criticism for their support of the U.S. Department of Education and U.S. Department of Justice seeking civil rights protections under Title IX for transgender people. The departments submitted a directive to public schools to secure civil rights for transgender students to allow them to utilize bathrooms and lockers room that align with their gender identities. The Obama Administration received political pushback after they threatened to withhold federal funding from states that refused to adhere to the directive. This led nearly 23 conservative states to file lawsuits in federal district court challenging that the Obama Administration was attempting to rewrite the definitions of sex, gender, and gender identity in the USA.

Months later U.S. District Judge Reed O'Connor temporarily blocked the directive contending that it misinterpreted the original intent of Title IX.[25] In a 38-page preliminary injunction, Judge O'Connor wrote that sex in the context of Title IX is, "the biological and anatomical differences between male and female students as determined at their birth."[26] The former Obama Administration's Department of Justice spokesperson said before his exit from the office that while they are "disappointed" in Judge O'Connor's decision, they were reviewing their options.[27]

Despite Obama's accomplishments for the larger LGBTQIA community, the election and presence of President Trump and Vice-President Pence have created a moral panic within the LGBTQIA community. Both have worked to overturn some of the most substantial LGBTQIA progress from the Obama Administration. Even with Trump promising to support the LGBTQIA community at the 2016 Republican National Convention, the bait and switch of political order is taking shape in his Administration. He said in his closing speech at the convention, "I will do everything in my power to protect our LGBTQ citizens from the violence and oppression of the hateful, foreign ideology."[28] However, this proclamation was only related to the protections of hate-based crimes and not equal rights for LGBTQIA people and their lives.[29]

On the first day of the Trump presidency, the White House LGBT page that housed major legislative accomplishments during the Obama Administration was removed. Weeks later the Trump Administration rolled back the Obama era guidelines of Title IX. The Administration indicated that the existing guidance under the Obama Administration did not "contain extensive legal analysis or explain how the position is consistent with the express language of Title IX, nor did they undergo any formal public process."[30] Months later he directed military officials to halt an Obama era plan to allow transgender people in the military. On Twitter he wrote:

> After consultation with my Generals and military experts, please be advised that the United States Government will not accept or allow Transgender individuals to serve in any capacity in the U.S. Military.[31]

Since his election to office, President Trump has appointed a number of cabinet members to his Administration that are affiliated with anti-LGBTQIA causes. Such appointments have sent an overt message that the overturning of most national LGBTQIA measures will be on the immediate and long-term agenda in the Trump Administration's quest to erase the LGBTQIA legacy of the Obama presidential era and restore a so-called normative gender order in the USA.

It is to be applauded that through the passage of LGBTQIA-friendly measures that the Obama Administration forced both white America and black America to face the fact that gender fluidity of all racial and ethnic minorities is becoming more of a societal, cultural, and gender norm. However, more work is needed to combat the visceral nature of the Trump presidency. To be agents of change against systemic and institutional circumstances, LGBTQIA people must work on two levels: First, as individuals actively participating in the process of change by educating themselves about the problem to find viable solutions. Second, on the institutional level, work must be done to educate political officials about the importance of equitable forms of protections for LGBTQIA people. Political officials, on both sides of the aisle, must work together despite ideological differences. Humanity must outweigh ideology. The increase in hate-based crimes against LGBTQIA people in recent years and spike after the election of President Trump should signal the need to find viable solutions for equal rights and protections.

The second recommendation is to transform the patriarchy that festers within the black community and culture leading black cisgender men to have primacy over black transgender women and facilitating toxic masculinity. hooks argues that "patriarchy is the single most life-threatening social disease assaulting the male body and spirit in our nation."[32] The narratives of this subset of black transgender women interviewed indicate that *some* black cisgender men are enablers of patriarchal violence. The compulsory toxic masculinity that exists in such men turns a blind eye to this societal and cultural issue and concern. When it comes to women in general, of all orientations and identities, this group of black cisgender men does not see them as individuals, but instead, a monolithic group that does not have the same societal and cultural privileges.

Followers of this patriarchal system of domination view these women in a single cubbyhole exposed to the wrath of their toxic masculine makeup. Such toxicity should not be aligned with the mass populace of black cisgender men. However, the latter group of black cisgender men who truly understand the value of the humanity of the black feminine position within the black community and in the larger American society must be equally culpable to limit black masculine silence and hold the former group more accountable.

This recommendation is no easy task but is imperative to fight against interpersonal circumstances that lead to violence. We cannot expect black cisgender men who have been raised under the religious-driven phobias constructed by the social institution of the black church that maintains secondary marginalization to easily shed their patriarchal belief and value system. However, as LGBTQIA activist, Timothy DuWhite, expressed, "As long as black trans-women remain oppressed and pushed to the margins we all remain oppressed and pushed to the margins."[33] This thinking reinforces that all black voices that resemble the diversity within the black community must be heard and their lives must matter if we are to achieve collective group actions that further the interests of blacks in American society.

The third recommendation is for the black community and culture to end the toxic silence and act as allies to be more accepting and inclusive of differing sexualities and gender identities. According to Lee and Kwan (2014, p. 130), "In the end, changing people's attitudes about transgender individuals is the best way to end the violence and discrimination that transgender people suffer." The ability to accept black transgender women as transcendent human beings and not as mere social, cultural, and political subjects would help to reduce such discrimination and violence and build trust with black cisgender people during an essential time in American history. Black cisgender people must be willing to interpret gender fluidity and complexity as a condition of normalcy and an opportunity to observe the presence of human beings whose life form extends beyond a traditional gender binary.

The idea of such acceptance and inclusiveness is not a novel idea, but a sign of societal and cultural transformation that centers on the generative power of black solidarity and the creation of safe spaces. For a culture to function to the best of its ability, the people within it have to work with each other for each other in the building of a collective consciousness. We must understand that transgender people, in general, are fighting battles each and every day against people whose experiences are grounded in the advent of power relations—patriarchy, heteronormativity, and socioeconomic status—thus, their interpretation of the lived experiences of transgender people is biased by their needs to establish fundamental differences rooted in dominance over acceptance and inclusiveness.

In sum, the task to provide equal rights and protections for transgender women has become increasingly urgent in the twenty-first century. The stories related to the transphobic violence and murders of these women have become too commonplace. The ongoing discussion about this epidemic needs to end with solution-based recommendations to preserve the humanity of transgender women. In the words of transgender activist Lourdes Ashley Hunter, who is the National Director of the Trans Women of Color Collective, "Every breath a black trans person takes is an act of revolution."[34] This declaration serves as the plea for radical change in a gendered American culture.

According to transgender activist, Janet Mock, in her 2017 empowering speech at the Women's March on Washington to promote transgender inclusion:

> I stand here today because of the work of my forebears, from Sojourner to Sylvia, from Ella to Audre, from Harriet to Marsha.
>
> I stand here today most of all because I am my sister's keeper. My sisters and siblings are being beaten and brutalized, neglected and invisibilizied, extinguished and exiled.
>
> Our approach to freedom need not be identical but it must be intersectional and inclusive. It must extend beyond ourselves.[35]

Mock's powerful words were directly analogous to the historical mission led by transgender pioneers such as Sylvia R. Rivera (1951–2002) and Marsha P. Johnson (1945–1992), who both were on the front line at the 1969 Stonewall Riots, to provide a voice for the equal rights and protections of transgender women. It is in her words that we understand, those who genuinely believe in the beauty of humanity must and will continue to fight for the liberation of all.

Notes

1. See @ Lavernecox (2016, November 9). Available at: https://twitter.com/Lavernecox/status/796414471157620736.
2. More information on the 2016 movie, *Moonlight*, is available at: http://www.imdb.com/title/tt4975722.
3. The following article highlights four black LGBTQIA people within the Black Lives Matter movement. See Dalton, D. 2015. "How 4 Black Lives Matter activists handle queerness and trans issues." *DailyDot.com*. Available at: http://www.dailydot.com/layer8/black-lives-matter-queer-trans-issues (October 11).
4. See the full 2016 press release from the U.S. Department of State about the Transgender Day of Remembrance (TDoR). Available at: https://www.state.gov/secretary/remarks/2016/11/264462.htm.
5. Black Trans Liberation Tuesday falls on the fourth Tuesday in August each year in an attempt to correspond with the death of the late black transgender activist, Marsha P. Johnson.
6. See Peoples, A. 2016. "Reflections on cis solidarity: One year after black trans liberation Tuesday." *GetEQUAL.org*. Available at: http://www.getequal.org/blog/reflections-on-cis-solidarity-one-year-after-black-trans-liberation-tuesday (August 26).
7. See Talusan, M. 2015. "Black Lives Matter calls attention to killed black trans women on national day of action." *BuzzFeed.com*. Available at: https://www.buzzfeed.com/meredithtalusan/black-lives-matter-trans-liberation-tuesday?utm_term=.sny4yaAvn#.ptwd6XM1D (August 26).
8. Ibid.
9. The entire online blog post titled, "Why black men must show up for trans-women of color" is available at: http://www.believeoutloud.com/latest/why-black-men-must-show-trans-women-color (August 28, 2015).
10. Ibid.
11. See Lamble (2008, p. 25) who counters this position and argues "that current manifestations of TDoR potentially limit the possibilities for resisting racialized gender violence in meaningful and effective ways."
12. See Willis, K. 2016. "Black trans liberation Tuesday must become an annual observance." *Rewire.com*. Available at: https://rewire.news/article/2016/08/23/black-trans-liberation-tuesday-must-be-annual (August 23).
13. See Jones, R. P., Cooper, B., Cox, D., and R. Lienesch. 2016. "Majority of Americans oppose laws requiring transgender individuals to use bathrooms corresponding to sex at birth rather than gender identity." *PRRI.org*. Available at: http://www.prri.org/research/lgbt-2016-presidential-election.
14. Ibid.
15. See Talbot, A. 2015. "The state of LGBT equality in America." *MSNBC.com*. Available at: http://www.msnbc.com/msnbc/the-state-lgbt-equality-america (January 18).
16. It is known that former Vice-President, Joe R. Biden Jr., who is an LGBTQIA ally, was the conscience for former President H. Obama on LGBTQIA rights and protections. Despite opposing same-sex marriage and only being in favor of civil unions early in his presidency, Obama described the marriage equality movement as "the fastest set of changes in terms

of a social movement that I've seen." See Levine, S. 2016. "Obama admits his daughters helped change his position on marriage equality." *The HuffingtonPost.com*. Available at: http://www.huffingtonpost.com/entry/obama-same-sex-marriage_us_571b9da4e4b0d-0042da96ea5 (April 23).

In 2012, Biden called transgender rights issues "the civil rights issue of our time."

See Grindley, L. 2016. "Yet Another Reason Joe Biden Is Everyone's Favorite LGBT Ally." *Advocate.com*. Available at: http://www.advocate.com/politics/2016/8/02/yet-another-reason-joe-biden-everyones-favorite-lgbt-ally (August 2).

17. See Condon Jr., G. E. 2014. "On gay rights, Obama has built a legacy." *TheAtlantic.com*. Available at: http://www.theatlantic.com/politics/archive/2014/06/on-gay-rights-obama-has-built-a-legacy/442659 (June 17).

18. See the full "Memorandum for the heads of executive departments and agencies on federal benefits and non-discrimination, 6–17–09." Available at: https://www.whitehouse.gov/the-press-office/memorandum-heads-executive-departments-and-agencies-federal-benefits-and-non-discri.

19. This clause, Section 1557, was updated in 2016 to improve health equity by adding gender identity. For more information, visit the U.S. Department of Health and Human Services. Available at: http://www.hhs.gov/about/news/2016/05/13/hhs-finalizes-rule-to-improve-health-equity-under-affordable-care-act.html. It is also important to note that at the state level Republican lawmakers have proposed legislation in the form of "Protecting Religious Freedom" that would deny LGBTQIA people access to healthcare based on religious beliefs.

20. It is estimated that more than 13,500 service members were dismissed under this policy.

21. See Montopoli, B. 2011. "Obama administration will no longer defend DOMA." *CBSNews.com*. Available at: http://www.cbsnews.com/news/obama-administration-will-no-longer-defend-doma (February 24).

22. The Executive Order amended Executive Order 11246, which was issued by former President Lyndon B. Johnson, adding sexual orientation and gender identity to the list of protected categories. For more information, the details of the Executive Order are available on the White House website: Available at: https://www.whitehouse.gov/blog/2014/07/21/president-obama-signs-new-executive-order-protect-lgbt-workers.

23. See the full transcript, "Remarks by the president on the supreme court decision on marriage equality, 6–26–15." Available at: https://www.whitehouse.gov/the-press-office/2015/06/26/remarks-president-supreme-court-decision-marriage-equality.

24. See Malloy, A., and K. de Vries. 2015. "White House shines rainbow colors to hail same-sex marriage ruling." *CNN.com*. Available at: http://www.cnn.com/2015/06/26/politics/white-house-rainbow-marriage (June 30).

25. For more information, see the full preliminary injunction order. Available at: https://www.texasattorneygeneral.gov/files/epress/Texas_et_al_v._U.S._et_al_-_Nationwide_PI_(08-21-16).pdf.

26. Ibid.

27. See Cohen, K. 2016. "Federal judge blocks Obama transgender bathroom directive for schools." *WashingtonExaminer.com*. Available at: http://www.washingtonexaminer.com/federal-judge-blocks-obama-transgender-bathroom-directive-for-schools/article/2599856 (August 22).

28. See Gittens, H. 2016. "Trump: 'I will protect our LGBTQ citizens.'" *NBCNews.com*. Available at: http://www.nbcnews.com/card/trump-i-will-protect-our-lgbtq-citizens-n614621 (July 21).

29. It should be noted that in 2012 at the Miss Universe pageant, at the time owned by Donald J. Trump, he initially disqualified Canadian Jenna Talackova from participating because she was a transgender woman. He later shifted his position after learning Talackova underwent SRS four years prior to the competition.

30. See the full two-page "Dear Colleague" letter addressed to public schools. Available at: http://fingfx.thomsonreuters.com/gfx/rngs/USA-TRUMP/010031ZW4JJ/Bathroom%20 Guidance%20Letter.pdf.

31. See @realDonaldTrump (2017, July 26). Available at: https://twitter.com/realDonaldTrump/ status/890196164313833472.

32. See hooks, b. 2004. "Understanding patriarchy." Available at: http://imaginenoborders. org/pdf/zines/UnderstandingPatriarchy.pdf.

33. Ibid.

34. See Hunter, L. A. 2015. "Every breath a black trans woman takes is an act of revolution." *HuffingtonPost.com*. Available at: http://www.huffingtonpost.com/lourdes-ashley-hunter/ every-breath-a-black-tran_b_6631124.html (February 6).

35. See L'Heureux, C. 2017. "Read Janet Mock's empowering speech on trans women of color and sex workers." *NYMag.com*. Available at: http://nymag.com/thecut/2017/01/read-jan-et-mocks-speech-at-the-womens-march-on-washington-trans-women-of-color-sex-work-ers.html (January 21).

References

Cohen, C. 1999. *The boundaries of blackness: AIDS and the breakdown of black politics.* Chicago: University of Chicago Press.

Cohen, C. 2014. Deviance as resistance: A new research agenda for the study of black politics. In T. L. Anderson (Ed.), *Understanding deviance: Connecting classical and contemporary perspectives* (478–495). New York: Routledge.

Lamble, S. 2008. Retelling racialized violence, remaking white innocence: The politics of interlocking oppressions in Transgender Day of Remembrance. *Sexuality Research & Social Policy* 5(1): 24–42.

Lee, C., and P. K. Y. Kwan. 2014. The trans panic defense: Heteronormativity, and the murder of transgender women. 66 *Hastings L. J. 77*; GWU Law School Public Law Research Paper No. 2014–10; GWU Legal Studies Research Paper No. 2014–10.

A P P E N D I X   A . 1

METHODOLOGICAL DETAILS

Interviews with Black Transgender Women

The interviews with black transgender women were conducted between September 14, 2015, and March 19, 2016, in Houston, Texas. A purposeful sample of nine participants was chosen through the snowball sampling method with assistance from local LGBTQIA groups and organizations, transgender activists, and social media outlets.

Approximately 23 black transgender women were contacted. Nine agreed to participate in the study. Six of the nine black transgender women interviewed work in the sex trade profession. The selection of these women was based on availability and not to further stigmatize transgender women as mere sex workers. As mentioned in Chapter 3, many transgender women are ostracized from the traditional workplace, which represents a labor issue and not a moral issue. Nevertheless, their lived experiences as transgender sex workers are not recorded in the context of painting the sex trade profession as a monolithic phenomenon for all transgender women. This book contends that transgender sex workers, and transgender women in general, are valuable members of our society and must not be labeled. Transgender women who work in this profession are exposed to harassment, forms of abuse, forms of violence, and murder more than other transgender women. Therefore, their participation, while being the most willing participants, was also imperative to provide an active voice to explain why these women are disproportionately victimized.

Participants ranged in age from 19 to 39. The average age was 27.2. All of the in-depth interviews were conducted face-to-face. Due to the nature and sensitivity of the study, many of the participants contacted were initially indecisive about taking part in the book. Eleven of the 23 women originally contacted requested a copy of the interview schedule to review the questions. The interview schedule was sent to them via email. Despite seeing the preliminary round of questions ahead of time, a number of the women declined. Even when interviewing participants face-to-face who consented to be apart of the book, it was essential to present to them the societal and cultural contribution of such a study, and as well, exhibit a level of sensitivity to overcome the initial concerns about exploitation.

At the beginning of the interviews, broader questions were asked to allow the participants the ability to speak freely and follow-up with more specific questions. This technique was useful for some participants but not all. Some of the participants still refused to answer questions and/or provided partial answers to questions. This was understandable due to the forms of discrimination and violence and overall negative circumstances experienced by these women. They were strongly encouraged only to share detailed experiences of discrimination and violence in which they felt comfortable describing to me.

The amount of information disclosed ultimately led to the decision to feature Sophie Rush, Mia Ryan, and Jessica Sugar in Chapter 4 as case studies due to the incredible openness of their responses in the interviews and willingness to allow participant observations as well. Despite some of the women not feeling comfortable with disclosing information about all facets of their lives, they all provided useful and important information to the formation of this book.

The black transgender women were interviewed using semi-structured, open-ended questions. Mia Ryan, who provided the first formal interview, examined the questions prior to using them with other participants. Her feedback was critical in constructing an interview schedule conducive to interviewing black transgender women. According to Berg (1998, p. 61), "this type of interview involves the implementation of a number of predetermined questions … in a systematic and consistent order, but the interviewers are allowed freedom to digress; that is, the interviewers are permitted to probe far beyond the answers." All interviews averaged around 45–60 minutes in length. The length of the interviews varied depending on the depth of the responses. Each participant was asked the same series of questions from the interview schedule. The interviews were digitally recorded. Once each interview was completed, they were transcribed and analyzed for common themes, topics of analysis, and trends.

Professional and ethical standards were adhered to in maintaining the confidentiality of the information provided. Black transgender women are considered a vulnerable research population that requires anonymity to safeguard their well-being. Two participants, Jae Palmer and Mia Ryan, granted permission to allow their legal names to be used in the book. The remaining seven participants chose to remain anonymous. In these cases, pseudonym names were used. I allowed participants to choose their own names. The anonymity of these research participants was maintained to allow full disclosure on questions. In social science research, it is important for participants to know that their responses if published will not be identifiable as their own (Robson 1995, p. 43). According to Mia Ryan, "Transgender women use different names depending on the situation. We have a legal name, street name, escort name, social media name, and email name."

Limitations

The selection of the pool of participants has limitations: First, a larger sample of black transgender women could have provided more insight into the lived experiences of these women. Second, the pool is limited to the city of Houston, Texas. Third, six of the nine black transgender women interviewed work in the sex trade profession. The selection of these women can potentially skew the results toward overemphasizing the negative circumstances of transgender women. Fourth, a small sample size and an oversample of women who work in the sex trade profession can possibly saturate the objectivity of the study (see Bernard 2011). Last, there were no questions asked related to their HIV/AIDS status.

Interview Schedule

Gender Identity

1. What is your current gender identity?
2. Do you consider yourself to be transgender?

3. When did you realize that you were different with regards to your gender identity?
4. Tell me about your transition and/or coming out.
5. How has your gender identity evolved over time?

Reaction from Family and Friends

6. What reaction have you received from family and friends?
7. What reaction have you received from members within the black community (besides family and friends)?

Black Masculinity and Femininity

8. Have you ever identified as a black cisgender man? If so, explain that time in your life before the transition.
9. What reaction have you received from black cisgender men for no longer identifying as a black cisgender man?
10. Do you ever identify as a black cisgender woman?[1]
11. Do members within the black community treat you different or similar to a black cisgender woman?
12. Do you believe most members within the black community identify you as a black cisgender woman?
13. How do black cisgender women react to you identifying as a cisgender woman?

Gender-Based Violence

14. Please tell me about a time that you may have experienced one or more of the forms of abuse and violence described. *The descriptions of verbal abuse, psychological abuse, physical violence, intimate partner violence, and sexual violence were provided.*
15. If you have experienced any of these forms of violence, did you report it to law enforcement officials?
16. What was the response and/or outcome of reporting the violence?
17. Do you believe that the forms of violence experienced were due to your gender identity?
18. How have you coped with these violence experiences? Have you ever sought professional help?

Transgender Violence and Murders

19. Why do you believe there is an increasing number of black transgender women being murdered within the black community and in American society?
20. Who are the individuals believed to be committing these murders? What is motivating their actions?
21. Do you believe that the black community and the Black Lives Matter (BLM) movement have fought for the humanity of black transgender women?

Violence and Murders in the Sex Trade Profession

22. What led you to work in the sex trade profession? (only if applicable)
23. What role do you believe that working as a transgender sex worker leads to transphobic violence and murders? (only if applicable)
24. Understanding the risks associated with this profession, how long do you wish to remain in the profession—or—do you believe that American society has not facilitated a societal and cultural environment that allows transgender women to gain traditional employment opportunities?

Table A.1. Demographic of Black Transgender Women Participants.

Names	Age	Legal Name	Occupation	Education
Bobbie Golden	27	N	Escort/Student	Some College
Arianna Gray	19	N	Student	Some College
Venus Love	31	N	Escort	High School
Naomi Mars	25	N	Escort	High School
Jae Palmer	20	Y	Retail Worker	Some College
Sophie Rush	39	N	Escort	College Graduate
Mia Ryan	29	Y	Beautician	Some College
Jessica Sugar	31	N	Escort	HS Drop Out
Alexandria Sweet	24	N	Escort	High School

Note: The interviews of black transgender women were conducted between September 14, 2015 and March 19, 2016.

A P P E N D I X   A . 2

CHAPTER 2: DATA AND METHODS

Black Men and Black Women Participants

Using a convenience, nonprobability sample of blacks in the greater Houston metropolitan area, the goal was to collect attitudinal data. This study administered a survey through the data collection site Survey Monkey (surveymonkey.com) to gauge black cisgender attitudes toward black transgender women.

The sample was collected from March 14, 2016 to March 18, 2016. Black respondents were asked via email by a popular urban club promoter in Houston to click on a link to the Survey Monkey questionnaire titled, "Attitudes about Black LGBTQIA People in Houston." The email contained a description of the intent of the study and definitions of the important terms. The club promoter was compensated for his electronic mailing list. The list contained approximately 1372 individuals. The final sample for this study was (N = 431). The black sample was (N = 315). The median time participants spent completing the entire questionnaire was approximately 18 minutes.

The study sample was predominantly women, 61% (265). Men made up 39% (166) of the sample. There was a higher percentage of blacks in the sample, 73% (315) in comparison to whites 19% (83), Hispanics 4% (19), and Asians 3% (14). The sample's mean age was 28.6 years, the median level of education attained was "some college," and median annual household income was between $30,000 to $39,999.

The black cisgender sample was (N = 279). Black cisgender women in the sample were 58% (161), and black cisgender men were 42% (118). The black LGBTQIA sample was (N = 36). There were 27 women and nine men. No other racial and ethnic group identified as a person within the LGBTQIA community. None of the respondents identified as transgender. LGBTQIA respondents were excluded from the analyses due to such a small sample size.

Instrumentation

Respondents were asked to complete a 19-question survey. They were asked their age, gender, education, income, and various questions related to black LGBTQIA people and black transgender people. Questions were constructed on a Likert scale. This type of scale measures whether the respondents have either positive or negative attitudes toward a statement. After completion of the survey, responses were summed to create a score for each question item.

The next step in the analysis was to conduct ordinary least squares models examining black cisgender acceptance of black LGBTQIA people and black transgender people. The dependent variables to measure black cisgender acceptance is based on the items from questions 12–14 (black LGBTQIA people) and 15–17 (black transgender people). The study summed responses to these items to form two composite measures of black cisgender acceptance. The alpha coefficients are 0.83 and 0.76 respectively, which are both indicative of scales with acceptable internal consistency.

Question Wording

Demographic Variable(s)

Questions 1–4: The demographic variables of age, gender, education, and income were employed in the study. Age is operationalized through the following question: "What is your age?" The scores on this response are ordinal and ranged from below 18 to 65+. Gender is a dichotomous variable. The variable is operationalized through the following question: "What is your gender?" (M = 1, F = 0) Education is operationalized through the following question:

"What is the highest grade of school that you have completed?" The scores on this response ranged from grade school to graduate/professional degree. Income is operationalized through the following question: "As you read some categories of income, please tell me your total family income." The scores on this response ranged from below $10,000 to over $100,000.

Religion

5. How important is the ideal of religion in your life today?
Very important = 1, Fairly important = 2, and Not very important = 3

LGBTQIA Status

6. Are you a member of the LGBTQIA community? If yes, please specify.
Yes = 1 and No = 0.
7. Are you transgender? If yes, please specify.
Yes = 1 and No = 0.

Contact with Black LGBTQIA

8. Have you ever had contact with a black LGBTQIA person?
Yes = 1, No = 0

Contact with Black Transgender

9. Have you ever had contact with a black transgender person?
Yes = 1, No = 0
10. Have you ever had contact with a black transgender man?
Yes = 1, No = 0
11. Have you ever had contact with a black transgender woman?
Yes = 1, No = 0

Dependent Variable

Black Acceptance

The measure of black acceptance is based on two groups of items. These items, listed in the order in which they were asked, are:

Black LGBTQIA Acceptance

12. Do you agree that the black church should condemn black LGBTQIA people? Response categories: 5. Strongly disagree; 4. Somewhat disagree; 3. Neutral; 2. Somewhat agree; 1. Strongly agree. The values of this question are in the reverse to coincide with the direction of the opinions of the respondents.
13. Do you agree that the combination of religious, moral, and ethical beliefs inhibit black Americans from accepting black LGBTQIA people? Response categories: 5. Strongly agree; 4. Somewhat agree; 3. Neutral; 2. Somewhat disagree; 1. Strongly disagree.
14. Do you agree that the black community should be accepting of black LGBTQIA people? Response categories: 5. Strongly agree; 4. Somewhat agree; 3. Neutral; 2. Somewhat disagree; 1. Strongly disagree.

Black Transgender Acceptance

15. Do you agree that the combination of religious, moral, and ethical beliefs inhibit black Americans from accepting black transgender people? Response categories: 5. Strongly agree; 4. Somewhat agree; 3. Neutral; 2. Somewhat disagree; 1. Strongly disagree.
16. Do you agree that the black community should be accepting of black transgender people? Response categories: 5. Strongly agree; 4. Somewhat agree; 3. Neutral; 2. Somewhat disagree; 1. Strongly disagree.
17. Do you agree that the black community should view black transgender women the same way we view black cisgender women? Response categories: 5. Strongly agree; 4. Somewhat agree; 3. Neutral; 2. Somewhat disagree; 1. Strongly disagree.

Perception of Black Transgender People

Write-in Question

18. What is your perception of black transgender men?
19. What is your perception of black transgender women?

Limitations

This study is not without limitations. There were several drawbacks: First, there was not an equal distribution of all races to maximize variance. Second, it was a relatively small sample size. Despite being a small sample size, it did provide an acceptable margin of error. Third, using a convenience, nonprobability sample of blacks from the greater Houston, Texas metropolitan area may not be generalizable to the mass black population. Fourth, the Likert scale only measures agreement or disagreement with a statement. There was no narrative for each individual response. Last, as with all surveys, it is impossible to know whether the respondents were truthful with their answers.

APPENDIX A.3

INTERVIEW OF FORMER HOUSTON, TX, MAYOR, ANNISE D. PARKER, DECEMBER 7, 2015

The interview with former Houston Mayor Annise D. Parker was facilitated through the Chief Policy Officer and Director of Communications, Janice Evans-Davis. On November 23, 2015, Ms. Evans-Davis was contacted and sent an interview request letter explaining the intent of the interview and mission of the book. Given that Mayor Parker was vacating the office on January 2, 2016, time constraints and political obligations made it was most convenient for her to respond via email. On December 7, 2015, Mayor Parker returned answered questions from the interview schedule.

Questions and Answers

1. Why do you believe the Houston Equal Rights Ordinance (HERO) failed to pass in the city of Houston?
HERO failed to pass because of a vicious and very effective opposition campaign that was based on lies. It was a prime example of the old adage about repeating a lie often enough.

2. In its current form, do you believe that HERO is a well-written ordinance?
Yes. HERO was crafted based on similar ordinances in effect in all other major cities. There have been some who have suggested that we should not have

included protections for transgender people. I could not support an ordinance that was not inclusive of all populations that need protections. There is not enough time for me to take the issue up again before I leave office, but Houston will have anti-discrimination protections in the not too distant future. The community will demand it.

3. Do you believe that voting against HERO was a form of discrimination against transgender people? If so, please explain.

Not necessarily. People voted against the ordinance simply because they believed the lies they were being told. They believed it would allow any man, at any time, to have access to women's bathrooms. The opposition's TV commercial showing a little girl being followed into the restroom by a man was very effective and capitalized on the fear that HERO would somehow make it easier for sexual predators to commit crimes.

The force behind this campaign is a very small minority in the local community that has been working against LGBTQIA rights for decades. They demonized transgender women for their own purposes.

4. Do you believe that the city of Houston is a safe social environment for members of the LGBTQIA community?

Of course. The vote on HERO is not at all reflective of what Houston really is. We are the most diverse city in the nation. We are open, tolerant and accepting of that which is different. We don't care who your parents are, where you came from or who you choose to love; we care about what you have to offer.

5. Why do you believe there is an increasing number of black transgender women being murdered in American society?

Society is still largely ignorant of what it means to be transgender. The economic and social impact of transitioning can be financially and psychologically devastating. Transgender women are often dehumanized, and the lack of knowledge means that societal taboos against harassing the minority are ignored. Too many transgender women are forced into the sex trade [profession], where they become particularly vulnerable targets.

6. Do you believe that governmental officials, at all tiers of government, are doing enough to protect the rights of transgender people?

We can never do enough to protect our vulnerable populations. Local protections like HERO can help because they provide a simpler avenue for residents to pursue when they believe they have been discriminated against. They can file a complaint without the need of a lawyer and a federal lawsuit.

Laws are necessary but not sufficient. The transgender community will have to follow the path of the gay and lesbian community: be out, be visible, be vigilant in fighting to preserve their rights.

Advocacy Information for LGBTQIA People.

Counseling Hotline	Suicide Hotline	Legal Assistance	Advocacy
LGBT National Help Center glbthotline.org (888) 843–4564	Trans Lifeline translifeline.org (877) 565–8860	Transgender Law Center transgenderlawcenter.org (415) 865–0176	Human Rights Campaign www.hrc.org (202) 628–4160
LGBT National Youth Talk line glbthotline.org (800) 246–7743	The Trevor Project Lifeline, for LGBT youth thetrevorproject.org (866) 488–7386	Sylvia Rivera Law Project srlp.org (212) 337–8550	The National LGBTQ Task Force thetaskforce.org (202) 393–5177
PFLAG— Transgender Network pflag.org/ transgender (202) 467–8180	LGBT Switchboard Houston www.montrosecenter.org/hub/services/avp/switchboard/ (713) 529–3211	Hate Crime National Hotline stoppingthehate.org/media.htm (206) 350–4283	National Center for Transgender Equality transequality.org (202) 642–4542
TransFamily transfamily.org (216) 691–4357	National Suicide Prevention Lifeline suicidepreventionlifeline.org/help-yourself/lgbtq/ (800) 273–8255	Lambda National Headquarters www.lambdalegal.org (212) 809–8585	Renaissance Transgender Association, Inc. www.ren.org (610) 636–1990

Note

1. It is important to state that even though "cisgender" refers to individuals whose gender identity matches their medically assigned sex, many of the black transgender women wanted to be considered a black cisgender woman during the interview process because that translated to a "real woman." The alternative to this question was, "Do you ever identify as a black woman?"

References

Berg, B. L. 1998. *Qualitative research methods for the social sciences, 3rd Edition*. Boston: Allyn and Bacon.

Bernard H. R. 2011. *Research methods in anthropology: Qualitative and quantitative approaches, 5th Edition*. Lanham: AltaMira Press.

Robson, C. 1995. *Real world research*. Oxford: Blackwell.

ABOUT THE AUTHOR

Dr. William T. Hoston, Sr., Ph.D., is a professor, author, motivational speaker, poet, and documentarian who hails from New Orleans, Louisiana. He is Associate Professor of political science at the University of Houston—Clear Lake. Dr. Hoston holds research interests in the areas of minority voting behavior, political behavior of Black politicians, race and minority group behavior, Black masculinity, sexualities and gender, race and crime, and theories and dynamics of racism and oppression. His work traverses multiple genres, including editorials, essays, fiction, and poetry.

Dr. Hoston is the author or editor of sixteen books; most recently, *Listen to Me Now, or Listen to Me Later: A Memoir of Academic Success for College Students*, 3rd Edition (2018); *Power to the People: Ascending Beyond Racism* (2018); *New Perspectives on Race and Ethnicity: Critical Readings about the Black Experience in Trump's America* (2018); *Race and the Black Male Subculture: The Lives of Toby Waller* (2016); *Real Niggas in Training* (2016, 2015); and *Black Masculinity in the Obama Era: Outliers of Society* (2014). He is currently finishing two academic book projects: *Acts of Mobilization and Activism: An Analysis of Modern-Day Campus Protests* and *Bobby Wright and Fred Hampton: Lives Intertwined*.

For more information on Dr. Hoston, please visit: www.WilliamHoston.com.

INDEX

W

X

Y

Z